Return of a Green Philosophy

Return of a Green Philosophy

THE WISDOM OF ÓÐINN, THE POWER OF ÞÓRR, AND FREYJA'S POWER OF NATURE

Rev. Dr. JC Husfelt

ISBN: 0692444513
ISBN 13: 9780692444511
Library of Congress Control Number: 2015912107
Snowy Owl, Port Ludlow, WA

For my family—
Sherry, Jamie, Jessie, and LilyRose,
the Bee Clan

I would like to express my love, gratitude, and appreciation to the earth, nature, its creatures, and the otherworld for experiences that no amount of gold could buy.

Contents

Foreword

This book is not an in-depth study of the Norse eddas and sagas. There are other authors who will provide you with an excellent in-depth exploration of them. It is interesting to note in Old Norse, *edda* means great-grandmother. In my experience this holds great meaning. In many indigenous cultures, the children are schooled more in life skills by the grandparents than the parents, specifically the grandmother. The rationale is that the parents are still learning life skills and need the wisdom of years. If we then use the term *great-grandmother* to identify a group of writings, it implies the literature has an element of great wisdom. I specifically delve into this wisdom, combining it with my knowledge and experience to provide a personal pathway to awaken to this wisdom, which I believe is based on primordial knowledge.

Right now, change and transformation are needed. A return to a *green philosophy* is needed. This is an egalitarian philosophy of humanity's partnership with the seen and unseen things of the earth and nature—a green philosophy. Furthermore, society has lost many of the values treasured by past indigenous cultures, such as a partnership with nature, truth telling, and elder/ancestor respect and honor. We need to discover meaning in life—not accumulate money and material things. The equality of men and women as well as the equality of all things—as all have the starlight/divine spark within them—needs to be reinstated. These and other lost values need to be reinstated throughout this earth. Nature needs to be respected, loved and cared for by humanity. We need to be partners in relationship with nature, not its stewards. The knowledge contained within this book will go a long way in making these things a reality. My wife, children, and I cannot do it alone. We need you, your family, your friends, and your community.

Rev. Dr. JC Husfelt, June 1, 2013

Introduction

deeply identify with Óðinn and Þórr. As a truth seeker like Óðinn, I have traveled for more than thirty years to different parts of the world, seeking wisdom and the myth, magic, and lore of elders and indigenous people. I have sacrificed self to self. My experience of listening, looking, and learning flowed from indigenous elders, healers, and shamans from all over the world. It also comes from my interactions with the young and old of other races and cultures, and emanates deeply from my own soul wisdom. This knowledge is what I refer to as "first knowledge."[1] It is knowledge that is woven throughout and found in all the first people's spiritual/religious traditions on this earth. This first knowledge has been referred to as *primordial knowledge* or the *Primordial Tradition (perennial philosophy)*. As such, it portrays universal themes, principles, and truths. In other words, "the term *Primordial Tradition* is utilized to describe a system of spiritual thought and metaphysical truths that overarches all the other religions and esoteric traditions of humanity."[2] Furthermore, "the perennial philosophy proposes that reality, in the ultimate sense, is One, Whole, and undivided—the omnipresent source of all knowledge and power. We do not perceive this reality because the field of human cognition is restricted by the senses. But the perennial philosophy claims that these limitations can be transcended."[3]

Mythically, primordial knowledge was extremely important to Óðinn as well, so much that he sacrificed one of his eyes (no doubt a great sacrifice of self to self)! After this sacrifice Óðinn was allowed to drink from Mimir's well and thus acquired primordial knowledge. Some say Mimir was the smith who made the sword Balmung for the dragon-slaying hero Siegfried; others say he was the giant who guarded the well of wisdom. "Mimir was known as the Wise One or the Rememberer. His name is related to the Latin *memor* (mindful) and *memorari* (to remember). He was regarded as an ally and teacher of Óðinn. His is the Well of Remembrance, from which Óðinn drinks in order to acquire knowledge of the past, of the origins of things."[4]

I've drank from the well and been gifted from my soul with this power. Due to my extensive firsthand experiences of the otherworld, my initiation within various indigenous shamanic cultures, and my direct experience of the old ways of these cultures, I have an understanding and knowing of the pre-Christian Germanic-Norse-Icelandic spiritual beliefs and practices.

Additionally, since the age of eighteen, I've been following a warrior-philosopher path. I was awakened to this path by two movies I viewed as a teenager: *The Vikings* and *The 300 Spartans*. Accordingly from my life's journey, I have followed a philosophical path of warriorship that is difficult and demanding. This pathway is best exemplified within the cultures of the ancient Greeks and the Norse. What they both have in common is the quality of being able to command oneself. This is a unique ability seldom sought in our present-day culture.

⚜

My relationship with Þórr extends back to my childhood and my fascination with thunder and lightning and the power of the storm. In my seeking, elders and shamans taught me the spiritual knowledge of thunder and lightning and its usage on earth through lightning-struck trees. Then there was the Visitation, a true story I briefly tell in chapter 1.

And yes, I do relate to Freyja as well. As you will see, I have a close relationship with the maiden. Even though my soul and personality is very warrior-like, I have awoken my feminine energy and embraced my femininity. Of course, Freyja also has a warrior's energetic essence and a sacred relationship with cats, both of which happen to be a part of my energetic self.

My feminine energy was awakened in 1988 within the confines of Machu Picchu. This was after I had almost died on the Inca Trail. Don Eduardo Calderon was the shaman or *curandero*, who was leading the spiritual and ceremonial work. Our ceremonial destination within Machu Picchu was the Pachamama Stone, a bastion of earthly feminine energy. It was here that

Eduardo would conduct the sacred plant ceremony using the medicine of the "magical cactus."

The following account I wrote many years ago:

As the wind picked up, rain lightly fell and lightning lit up the darkened sky above us, and Eduardo set up his mesa in front of the gigantic mother stone and prepared to call in the guardian spirits of the four winds. He had placed his variously size and shaped power staffs and swords in the ground in front of his mesa cloth—Owl Staff, Serpent Staff, Eagle Staff, Hummingbird Staff, Saber of Saint Michael. There were other staffs as well, such as the Staff of the Maiden, the Virgin. I mention this staff in particular due to the fact that it was presented to me to use in the night ceremony. This was an appropriate staff for me for many reasons, one being that I was born under the sign of the Virgin—Virgo.

This magical staff was spiritually connected to the sacred highland lagoons and was made from black *chonta* wood. It would awaken the nurturing power and feminine energy within me, which I needed to accept. This would balance the strong male energy that I had and would help bring me into a state of inner balance and oneness.

Eduardo knew that I was also a teacher of the mystical warrior arts, as was he. He knew that it was not any of the warrior staffs, but the Staff of the Maiden that would bring me back into balance. He also knew that I needed the sacred power of the great earth mother stone—the Pachamama.

As others received various staffs and went off to different spots to do their work, I was assigned to the Pachamama stone along with one of the females in our group. One at a time, we would go in front of Eduardo to receive our staffs. It was at that moment when I would have my first taste of the otherworldly magical cactus as well. As I looked into Eduardo's eyes, he handed me a seashell filled with liquid.

"This is lovingly referred to as 'nose juice,'" Alberto said as he assisted Eduardo. "Put the shell to your nose, tilt your head back, and let the juice run down the back of your throat. Breathe, and if you start choking, stomp your foot."

Breathe, stomp my foot, imbibe a magical elixir through my nose... I would later learn that it was a mixture of herbs, black tobacco, and alcohol that was a powerful stimulant that would open the third eye and affect the various visionary centers of the brain.

It was definitely difficult to swallow, and I did stomp my foot, which helped. It was absolutely a rush. As I handed the shell back to Eduardo, I noticed that his eyes were black pools of focused intent.

"This is the visionary cactus juice, the San Pedro," Alberto stated as Eduardo handed me a small liquid-filled glass.

As soon as I finished drinking the potion, I danced over to the Pachamama Stone. We were asked to dance after taking the San Pedro for a reason I was still trying to figure out. But my focus was not on the dance or the reason for it; it was on the anticipated effects of the magical potion.

I waited and waited, but nothing really happened. Letting go of any further expectations, I settled in and focused my intent on the staff and my connection with the stone's great feminine energy. Time seemed to be suspended as I closed my eyes and attempted to become one with the Mother Stone.

How long I was a part of the otherworld, I do not know. But when I opened my eyes, the rain had stopped, the stars were shining brightly, and I had an insight. I had never been close to my own mother. In fact, in my mind, I had been raised by my grandmother. I had also always felt that my parents were not my parents.

My insight was that I had just reestablished a bond and had become closer to my mother—that is my other mother, mother earth, Freyja, the mother of us all. *Will this be an opening to my feminine side?* I wondered.

A few weeks later, my wife, Sherry, provided the answer. As I stepped off the plane in Portland, Maine, Sherry walked right past me, not recognizing me. When I spoke her name, she turned and some of her first words were, "You've changed." And I had; I had awakened my feminine side—the sacred marriage within had been consummated.

Philosophy

The word *philosophy* comes from the Greek φιλοσοφία (*philosophia*), which literally translates as "love of wisdom." Wisdom derives from the following formulas: information without experience remains just information: I = I; information combined with experience results in knowledge: IE = K; wisdom flows from the combination of knowledge and its experience: KE = W. Experience is the source.[5] Experience rewires the brain. In the following pages, you will combine knowledge with experience on your journey seeking the wisdom of Óðinn, the power of Þórr, and the power of nature, symbolized by Freyja.

Green Philosophy

As I stated in the foreword, a return to a green philosophy is needed. This is an egalitarian green philosophy of humanity's partnership with the seen and unseen things of the earth and nature. This concept played an important role in the Norse-Germanic mind. They were one with nature, respecting it and caring for it.

The gods and goddesses were, of course, important, but they were thought of as being distant, not directly involved in the everyday lives of the people. However, they still needed to be honored and given recognition.

On the other hand, earth and nature spirits overall played an important role in people's everyday lives. These were the dwarves, the elves, *huldufólk* (hidden people), trolls, and *landvættir* (land wights). In the Viking mind, there was a connection between all aspects of life—the seen as well as the unseen.

⚜

The following is excerpted from an article concerning the Norse religious practices of Iceland´s early Viking settlers by Neil McMahon:

Hardly a day goes by without the media presenting some grim new findings as to how the world's ecological environment is on the brink of imploding and that if there isn't a radical and immediate change in how we think and live our lives on this planet, then Doomsday is a mere few decades down the road.

Two major contributing factors as to why we seem so complacent about these constant warnings are firstly how divorced an ever-growing urbanized world has become from the natural environment, and secondly our increasing failure to nurture an inner spiritual self.

For centuries, Christianity preached that Man was the supreme ruler and the earth's resources were his for the taking. This Christian worldview encouraged Europe's aggressive drive to dominate and exploit nature in a spirit of complete indifference. With the Bible in one hand and a sword or gun in the other, indigenous peoples were conquered, empires built, and the Western world rode the wave of the Industrial Revolution and so-called progress. Granted, industrialization brought many advances, but it all came at a terrible price, both to the environment and that existentialist sense of soullessness that so often haunts us in the first world.

Science and technology alone are not going to get us out of the present ecological mess; we need to reconnect spiritually with the larger whole of reality. Unfortunately, mainstream institutionalized religions seem incapable of offering such a holistic perspective; however, many ancient indigenous religions do, and we should be looking to them for ideas and inspiration.[6]

In other words, the green philosophy of the Norse-Germanic people needs to return and to be embraced by us for the sake of our children and their children's children and all the creatures and things of the earth.

The Christian Usurpers

There are various sources for the multitude of problems and dysfunctions affecting humanity's body and soul. Two of the causes are institutionalized religion and capitalism. In many ways the primary source, which is the dysfunction of both institutionalized religion and capitalism, is the inequality of men and women (with men superior and women inferior) and the destruction of nature, the earth's biosphere.

We live in a patriarchal world. The entrenched mind-set of our culture is one of superiority to nature, of being a steward. This mind-set reflects the patriarchal view of nature, the feminine, as below or inferior to man. Accordingly, men know what is best in managing nature—the feminine. By its definition, *stewardship* implies inequality, with the male side of the duality being superior to the female/Mother Nature side. To put it in perspective, I am not a steward of my wife but her partner. Life is not about stewardship but about partnership. Stewardship is separation, while partnership is unity. My wife and I are not separate from each other but are together in unity as we journey through life.

As a society and culture, our separation from nature underlies many of the problems that we face today, from climate change to the worldwide abuse and second-class citizenship of women. There are multitudes of examples of the male-dominated religions controlling (or is it dominating?) women's bodies, through controlling their reproductive health and sexual activity. These range from the covering of the head and/or female body in Islam to birth control being a sin in the Catholic Church. These examples even extend to the founding and subsequent history of Iceland. The land of fire and ice was founded by the Norse in the ninth century, after the courageous Norse pagan purists left Norway to escape the Christian tide that was overwhelming pagan cultures and religions. In their new homeland, their freedom of body, mind, and spirit only survived about two hundred years until their Althing, the oldest surviving parliamentary institution in the world, declared Christianity the religion of Iceland. As a concession to the Norse pagans, their beliefs and practices were allowed to go underground. The point of this is that before the Church took over Iceland, men and women were equals in that society. The primary crime was blood feud. After the Church established its dysfunctional beliefs, women were regarded as inferior to men and the most frequent crime was incest. Men now owned all women's bodies.

❧

Due to the Christian incursion and conversion of the Norse-Germanic people, one of our sources in our attempts to discover the beliefs, myths, and rituals of the pre-Christian Norse is the *Prose Edda*. It comes not from the Norse pagans but from a Christian, Snorri Sturluson (1179–1241), an Icelandic historian, poet, lawyer, and politician. Herein lays the problem: If our knowledge is not coming directly from pagan/heathen sources, what is truth? And what is filtered through Christian dogma, doctrine, and the author's belief system and prejudices? We have the same problem with deciphering the Bible.

We do not know Snorri's true allegiance or beliefs. He is generally thought of as a Christian, but was he a pagan in spirit or both pagan and Christian? He seems to have had a caring respect for the tales of his people. Whichever he was, pagan and/or Christian, he still needed to present his *Prose Edda* in a form that would not offend the Church or go against its dogma. There may be truth and hidden knowledge within the *Prose Edda* as in the Bible; it just needs to be discovered—we need to separate the mead from the mash.

The other primary source of knowledge is the *Poetic Edda*, or the *Elder Edda*. The *Elder Edda* is a gathering of Old Norse poems mainly preserved in the Icelandic mediaeval manuscript *Codex Regius*. In my mind, it is purer, but the problem here lies in translating the Old Norse, especially names and their meanings and symbolism. This is a common problem we face in deciphering information and knowledge from elder written sources.

In addition to the eddas, we have the prolific Norse sagas. These are tales and legends of heroic and not so heroic deeds; of revenge, honor, and glory; of vows taken and vows broken; and of mythic heroes and epic battles. "A distinctive characteristic of the sagas is the objective narrative approach. Often the sagas describe events in great detail, including what was said by those involved. But they do not describe their inner life. Instead, the characters of the sagas reveal themselves through their words and actions."[7] A well-known saga is the Icelandic *Njáls saga*—*Brennu-Njáls saga* or *Burnt Njál*—the story of the burning of Njál. This is a tale of a blood feud lasting fifty years. These sagas can teach us and provide us with insight into human nature and life, in all its shades.

Concerning the relationship between gods and giants, according to Jón Hnefill Aðalsteinsson, "the mythological poems of the Edda have to be considered the most valuable sources of information on the giants in Old Norse mythology, and the relations between the giants and the gods. Next come the poems of Egill Skallagrímsson and those other named poets of the ninth and tenth centuries who refer to these subjects in their works. Snorri's *Prose Edda* comes in third place, followed by the *fornaldarsögur*, and finally the latter-day folk tales."[8]

❖

In seeking wisdom and power, the key to truth, which is personal, does not solely or completely lie in the written word or in historical and anthropological/archeological discoveries. Truth does not purely flow from the written or even the spoken word. And it surely does not come by being an observer of religious/spiritual/shamanic practices or by following a religion's dogma. But it does originate by being a participant who has had physical spiritual/mystical experiences of this world and the otherworld. In this manner, you will be able to separate the mead from the mash. You will not believe or have faith—you will know!

Consciousness

What is consciousness? It seems the answer to this question is as slippery as an eel or as difficult to hold on to as a moonbeam. "Explaining the nature of consciousness is one of the most important and perplexing areas of philosophy, but the concept is notoriously ambiguous."[9] But I'm going to make it less so. Consciousness is the sixth element. This makes it no less ambiguous than fire; fire is an element and so is consciousness.

However, consciousness as the sixth element is, in reality, divine consciousness. And this element of divine consciousness interpenetrates the other five elements of earth, water, fire, air, and space. In other words, divine consciousness is within all things in both the seen and unseen worlds. All things are conscious and aware—and this means all, not only creatures but such things as trees and even the earth itself. We are all one, all conscious and aware. In the Norse tradition, this divine consciousness may be symbolized by Óðinn, the AllFather.

Thus, divine consciousness is a consciousness of oneness. This is not the thought of oneness but the consciousness of it. In other words, our thoughts flow from our consciousness, and our thoughts determine our reality—as we think, we become.

We are born with a consciousness of oneness, but within an unknown period of time, it is overshadowed by a dualistic consciousness. This is the reason why the majority of people have a dualistic consciousness, which also means their thought patterns are dualistic—right and wrong, good and evil, win and lose, success and failure, and so on. If you have awakened to radical nonduality, where spirit and matter interpenetrate, your consciousness will be nondualistic as will be the thoughts that flow from your consciousness.

Our life quest is to reclaim our initial birth consciousness, a consciousness of oneness, which is referred to as "awakening."[10] As we awaken, we shift our consciousness and thought patterns from being dualistic to a reality of radical nonduality.

We can be assured that Snorri's consciousness was dualistic. He was a Christian following dogma and doctrine based on dualistic thinking—Heaven and Hell, God and the devil. Therefore, we need to approach his edda with the understanding that his writings reflect dualistic thought patterns flowing from a dualistic consciousness.

A cautionary tale in recent history is Jung and his theories and writings. "His ontology seemed often to be dualistic, as well as persistently ambiguous, and was necessarily so because the science of his day could not envision a nondualistic conception of spirit and matter."[11] Jung's consciousness was dualistic, which led him to an inaccurate conclusion in his concept of a collective unconsciousness. There is not a collective unconsciousness, which is a human psychological inheritance, but a consciousness that is divine and contained within all things of creation. Trees are alive; listen, and they will speak to you—only then can you speak to them, since you have listened to them first.

Pagan/Heathen

This book is a benefit to all people, but especially ones following the path of pagan and heathen traditions. However, this is not a Reconstructionist manual or a handbook to ritual and ceremony. It is a guide to commanding oneself by providing a journey of self-discovery through primordial knowledge and assisting in returning a green philosophy to the hearts and minds of people. It is a sacrifice; the path is not easy. But we would not want an easy path if we have the spirit of Óðinn within us. And we do. Óðinn is Allfather.[12] This means that the energy of Óðinn is within us and all things of creation. Seek now and discover how to awaken this energy.

Approach

I approach the deciphering of the Norse-Germanic tradition and mind-set from an experiential standpoint. One of the shamanic lineages my wife and I hold is an indigenous, First Peoples Coast Salish tradition of British Columbia, Canada. Additionally, after fifty years in the martial arts—not competitive but "battle" arts—I have a knowing of a traditional warrior's—not soldier's—mentality. Add to this my direct physical, sensory experiences of the otherworld.

The Coast Salish and the Norse are very closely intertwined. Both lived in longhouses; both are gift-giving cultures; both are coast dwellers; both have "god poles"; both are warrior and fishing based; both use *seiðr* and *galdr*; both have the concept of a *fylgja*; both *blot,* which the Salish call a burning; and both have similar environments (mythology, folklore, ceremonies, and ritual are highly environmentally driven and influenced). This is my approach in the writing of this book.

⚜

My wife and I began our seeking in 1981 in England and Scotland, when the sacred sites were, shall we say, virgin. Today, the Tor[13] in Glastonbury, England, is overwhelmed with tourists and New Agers. In 1981, it was only us and the sheep on the Tor. Since we were seeking surviving indigenous shamanic knowledge, in a few years, we turned our focus to the Hawaiian Islands, and North, Central, and South America. Our journey also took us to Japan, where I experienced a descending spirit exorcism on Kōyasan, a sacred, esoteric Buddhist mountain.

In all of our non-European journeys, we were still outsiders just as much as when we were the only nonnatives in a British Columbia longhouse during their winter spirit dancing. There was only one reason why we were allowed into the longhouse and not harmed: we were with two of our teacher's—Northwest Coast Salish shamanic elders who were respected and still feared by their people. No matter who we were with, it was still scary.

Over the years, we turned our focus back to our Northern European heritage as carriers of first knowledge and shamanic lineages. We can admire and learn from other cultures, but for many of us, we still lack a total sense of belonging to them. Even though I was born in America, I still carry a Northern European Scottish Norse bloodline. This is my cultural heritage, which I now present to you with the underpinning of thirty-plus years of experience of the first knowledge of other cultures' spiritual practices and traditions.

Do not ask why, but only experience from the depths of your soul
the mystery, and you will know; but will you ever know?

Raven, creator to some, evil to others,
Earthbound, injured wing, can't you fly?
Why, if divine, where comes the suffering?
Do you remember flying high, voice of power—black, or was it white?
Why maimed, earthbound, separate from heaven?

"Black to some is life, while white is death.
Experience the mystery for yourself," Raven shouts.
"Why do you refuse to see the mystery within me?
Always looking, judging, separating, but never seeing the light of the
mystery.
You do not know me; I am Raven,
The majestic one that suffers and weeps
For the ones I have left behind.

"What is life to one as me?
Surprise will be my answer to you.
I am not what I appear;
I am you, and you are me.
We are one."[14]

Return of a Green Philosophy Seeking Wisdom and Power

*"Let the tree stand, leave the moss on the rock,
and don't kill the fly on the window."*
—Allsherjargoði Sveinbjörn Beinteinsson

CHAPTER 1

Knowledge and Wisdom-Based Knowing

The majority of written works covering subjects ranging from spirituality, religion, and mythology to a culture's past beliefs and practices are based on historical, archeological, and anthropological study with a strong dose of left-brain, linear thinking thrown into the mix. Many times, these works are presented through the authors' own agendas, biases, and, of course, belief systems. Another factor prevalent throughout these works is the author as observer and not as a participant in the subject matter explored. Making sense of written information based on oral teachings and mythologies hundreds and thousands of years old is a practice in futility unless we have experienced the subject matter for ourselves—not as an observer but as a participant.

For example, baptism is one of the major sacraments of Christianity. It is a Christian initiation, a granting of grace, an entrance into the holy arms of the Church, and thus one's salvation. This ritualistic practice has nothing to do with sanctification. But even more important, baptism was not practiced by Jesus. Instead, he bathed people, which was a shamanic rite of sanctification and rebirth. Yes, we do have the born-again rites of certain sects of conservative Christians. In these born-again rituals conducted during the light of day, the officiates lay a person down into the water like they are in a coffin and then pull them back to an upright, standing position. All I can think of is that they have watched too many Bela Lugosi's Dracula movies.

Contrary to the dogma and doctrine of Christianity, I *know* the bathing practice of Jesus. It was totally different from the Christian ceremonial rites.

It involved submersion before the first light of day in living waters, such as a swift-flowing stream or river. It simulated drowning by a person swatting underneath the surface of the river three times. This was individually done in the nude, without anyone assisting you in the river.

Ritualistic immersion in running water (stream/river/waterfall) or the ocean is one of the oldest forms of symbolic death and rebirth and the sacrifice of self to self.[15] It is one of the essential steps in awakening. It is frightening but necessary. We need to physically and symbolically die in regards to the old to be born again—it is our second birth. It doesn't bring membership into an earthly or religious institution. It is the beginning of an awakening to our personal truths—those of the world and our authentic selves.

Few in the world still practice, teach, and conduct this form of purification. Outside of the Mandeans of the Middle East, the greatest concentration of dawn bathers are to be found within the indigenous communities that still practice and adhere to the old ways. There are few still alive who can initiate and put people into the living waters of the earth.

I am blessed to be one of those who still practices and initiates people into bathing. My modern-day John the Baptist[16] taught me this practice and passed on the power and authority to conduct bathing for others.

Worldview

To the Norse-Germanic consciousness, body (material, of this world) and soul (spirit, of the otherworld) were not stand-alone dualistic concepts but were united. If you picked up a stone, you were not only holding its body, but you were also embracing its essence, its soul. Everything has a soul/spirit within its material form. In other words, spirit and matter interpenetrate where everything has a divine spark/fire and consciousness within it. Everything is alive and conscious. This philosophy of the blending of spirit and matter is considered a worldview. This concept of the interpenetration of spirit and matter is called *radical nonduality*. It is my worldview and philosophy of life.

There is another insight into the Norse-Germanic worldview. Indigenous religions, such as the Norse-Germanic, "are local, earthbound, and this-worldly. Compelling evidence can be assembled to support the contention that indigenous cultures recognize no division between the 'secular' and the 'sacred.'"[17] Furthermore, as I state very clearly in *Do You Like Jesus—Not the*

Church?, Christianity was, and still is, a dualistic religion. According to Bil Linzie, "The heathen first hearing about the doctrine of dualism must have thought the Christian leaders/teachers to be very confused, perhaps even mad. For the heathen, as evidenced in both literature and burial practice as well as philology, the soul was the animating force of the body and could not therefore be separated from the body."[18]

If this was indeed the worldview of the pre-Christian Northern European cultures, then it stands to reason that written material and archaeological discoveries would best be viewed through the prism of radical nonduality. This premise could help explain burial practices and the importance of gods, goddess, and the many other supernatural beings and magic. Furthermore, can we make sense of the mysteries of this world and the otherworld without relying on the written word and artifacts? Yes, through the experience of nature (seen and unseen).

⚜

There is an ancient worldview of the "one and many." This concept extends as far back as the ancient Egyptians and Greeks. In simplified terms, this ancient philosophy of unity and multiplicity, or the "one and many," means that the one god, God or the Divine, is in all things, and all things are in the Divine. In other words, spirit is within matter, and matter is within spirit; both mutually penetrate. Thus, reality is interpenetrating radical nonduality—oneness. According to Vilhelm Grönbech: "In primitive religion, all question of monotheism or polytheism is idle, because there is no footing in the facts for the dilemma which is evolved from the contrast between Hellenism and Christianity. The divine power may manifest itself as one or as many according to circumstances."[19]

Dualistic Identity of the Nondualistic Otherworld

As a spiritual and religious philosopher, I deal in mysteries and the knowledge that the spiritual is accessible through the natural. Primarily, these are the mysteries of the otherworld and its interaction with our seen world. My foundational philosophical principle as well as worldview is radical nonduality—the interpenetration of spirit and matter, the absolute (male) and relative (female).

Reality is nondualistic even though our sense perception is dualistic. With this being true, the otherworld is nondualistic as well. So what happens to the concept of gods and goddesses?

They can still be perceived in this manner. For example, I identify my wife as a divine human being who just happens to be female. First and foremost, she is a divine human being with one of her intrinsic identities being female. Just as I am a divine human being, my masculinity is more prevalent and apparent than my femininity. But I still have both energies that blend within me. It then makes sense that we may identify these otherworldly but real sentient beings as leaning more toward a god, or goddess, identity.

In attempting to decipher the knowledge left to us from the Norse-Germanic traditions, we have to endeavor to distinguish between universal powers, such as sound or vibration, and actual otherworldly beings, whether they are named gods, goddesses, or hidden ones, such as elves and faeries. Since the otherworld and our world interpenetrate, nature's mountains and valleys, jungles, forests and glades, streams and rivers, oceans and seas are the best places in which to experience the presence and essence of the otherworld and its inhabitants. In other words, the otherworld will speak to us through nature and the power and force of earth and sky. We do not worship these places and forces but honor and bless them in our journey toward enlightenment. These powers and forces will help us through our various struggles in life. In this way, we are in partnership with them and nature. This partnership will bring balance and harmony to us and to our kin.

Reincarnation

One of the great mysteries of life is not about life at all but death. Mystery swirls around our physical death, even though it is inevitable. The question that enters everyone's mind at some point in their lives is: What happens after we die? Do we spend an eternity with seventy-two virgins? Or do we wait somewhere (not sure where) for the Rapture or the resurrection of our physical body?

Organized religions have utilized resurrection to their benefit by keeping people in fear and servitude. If people believe this propaganda of their church, temple, or mosque, then they are locked into being a slave of the religion. If they are Christians, then their behaviors will take on a philosophy wherein it doesn't really matter who or what they hurt and abuse through their actions, as they are guaranteed resurrection and a place in heaven due to their professed belief in the redeeming power of Jesus Christ.

A Christian's emphasis is on words, prayer, not on action, deeds. A deranged gunman can kill nine people while reloading his gun five times while no one physically stops him but only attempting to talk him out of his intrinsic evil rampage. We can see the dangers inherent in the church's emphasis on words/prayer not deeds and their concept of resurrection.

If resurrection is not reality, then what is? Reincarnation is a philosophical paradigm that causes shock and awe in Christian and Muslim circles. It is a threat to the power of organized religion. Early on, the Church of Rome saw the danger in people's belief in reincarnation. Consequently, "Those early Church Fathers who taught or believed in reincarnation were declared heretics, excommunicated, and their books were burned. Other heretics faced horrible deaths, such as being burned alive. Why? Think about it. If you believe you will reincarnate in another body, you cannot be controlled by fear of an eternity in the fires of hell.

"The church existed to hold power over the people, to tell them what to believe rather than have them think for themselves. Control by fear is not possible if an individual knows who she/he is (astrology) and that he will reincarnate again and again. There is nothing to fear when we know Truth; therefore, Truth must be hidden from the people."[20]

⚜

There are indications of a belief in reincarnation/rebirth within the Norse consciousness. Within the *Poetic Edda*,

> There are references to rebirth in the Helgi poems. The lovers Helgi and Sváva are said in the prose note at the end of *Helgakviða Hjörvarðssonar* to be born again, while at the close of *Helgakviða Hundingsbana II* there is a reference to a similar tradition about the later Helgi:

> It was believed according to ancient lore (*í forneskju*) that folk were reborn; but this is now said to be old women's lying tales. Helgi and Sigrún

are said to have been reborn; he was then called Helgi Haddingjaskati and she Kara Hálfdanardóttir, as is related in *Káruljóð*; and she was a Valkyrie.[21]

One of the most detailed accounts of Norse funeral rites was by the Arab diplomat Ahmad ibn Fadlán. Hidden in his account is the Norse belief in rebirth. Part of the rites involved the sacrifice of a servant girl. Before she was to die, she "was given a hen. She cut off its head and the body was thrown into the funeral ship. It is possible that birds of this kind symbolize rebirth…We may also think of the cock, Salgofnir, awakening the fallen warriors in Valhöll."[22]

It makes sense to recognize rebirth in the mind of the Norse. This "conception of rebirth combines, as it were, the idea of the indestructible soul and the close connection of this with the body after death."[23] Thus, we see the importance of grave mounds and sacred hills such as Helgafell Mountain in Iceland. "*Landnámabók* gives a number of references to certain Icelandic families who believed that after death they would pass into some particular hill or mountain near their home, showing that this belief, if it really flourished in late heathen times, was closely bound up with special localities, and with the unity of the kindred."[24] In regards to the grave mound, it seems possible "that the emphasis on the help and wisdom to be won from the world of the dead by the seeker who knows the way is based on a belief in the nearness and potency of the other world, prevalent in Scandinavia in pre-Christian times."[25] Furthermore, it was believed that "One can recognise a hero of the past in one's contemporary, by his courage, and by the contents and strength of his honour, but also his career provides its evidence, and this perhaps of the clearest, as to the connection between past and present."[26]

Of course, the Norse weren't the only ones who believed in reincarnation. Even in the New Testament, Jesus relates that John the Baptist was the reincarnation of the prophet Elijah. A belief in reincarnation is extremely important. It frees us from dogmatic religious beliefs and practices that seek to control people through fear, coercion, and intimidation. From a practical as well as a spiritual/religious viewpoint, believing in reincarnation is paramount to our soul's well-being and to the welfare of the earth and all its creatures.

⚜

So what does happen after we physically die? I believe that we pass over to the realms of the otherworld. Our human bodies are mortal, but our souls are immortal. I believe in reincarnation and that there is consciousness in the otherworldly realms.

Each one of us has an otherworldly lineage—an otherworldly DNA based on previous lives, and an earthly lineage (parental DNA). With this belief, racial prejudice has no relevance or foothold. "In the ancient world, the metaphysical views of the immortality of the soul and reincarnation often went hand in hand. The one was seen, in some ways, to justify the other as may be observed as major subjects in Plato's *Meno, Timaeus*, explicitly described in *Republic X* and elsewhere."[27]

Let's compare a belief in reincarnation to Christianity's dogma that, after a single lifetime, death will result in the gift of Heaven or the punishment of Hell. This dogma subtly insinuates that we are not responsible for the future well-being of the land or the earth and its creatures or future generations, as we will not reincarnate back on earth in a future time. As we are observing in this twenty-first century and in past centuries, this belief has opened a Pandora's box of ecological destruction spearheaded by the Church and capitalism.

If we look back in time, we discover:

By the seventh century, the Church had rewritten Catholic dogma to obliterate most of the original teachings of esoteric Christian groups such as the Essenes…Most importantly, they edited out all references to the universal doctrine of reincarnation, a central theme throughout Eastern religion as well as Druidic and early Christian life.

This had a profound effect on all succeeding ages. Before, people believed that their ancestors were still alive in the otherworld, and that, like themselves, they would be reborn into the group or tribe to which they belonged. In this way, warriors felt it an honor to die in order to protect their people. But there was a deeper responsibility; if you were to be reborn, then the land must be preserved not only for your children, but for yourself when you returned. Short-term exploitation would have been inconceivable. You and your children were, in a very real sense, the land.

The replacement of this with a "one-way trip" to heaven or hell forever changed people's attitude as it permeated into everyday life.

Under this doctrine that this life was the only one you were ever going to experience, it eventually became acceptable to seize as much as was possible in the short time available. The development of this impulse in recent times may be held to be directly responsible for many of the critical dilemmas facing the world today...

How far we have come from the ways of antiquity can be shown by our approach to the land in which we live. Today we think nothing of changing the essential features of the countryside in an effort to maximize the yield we may achieve from it or to make living more efficient, even if it blights the lives of those around and has unforeseen and unknowable consequences.[28]

Climate change is real; ecological destruction is great and ongoing. The oceans are becoming more acidic, providing an environment that is not friendly or healthy to its residents; however, there is hope: a shift in belief from resurrection to reincarnation will not immediately solve our problems, but in the long run, it will greatly help. What is your belief about what happens after physical death: finality, resurrection, or reincarnation? For myself, I do not believe; I know that one of the laws of creation is reincarnation. And otherworldly beings play a very important part in my knowing. Not only do I know the truth of reincarnation, but I know the truth of gods, goddesses, angels, or whatever label you would like to assign to these energetic beings of the unseen otherworld.

One last point: the Norse believed in Valkyrjar—female psychopomps or guides for the dead. I believe as well, and my belief is also based on my knowing. I will tell my tale about my experience of Valkyrjar in chapter 5.

My Knowing

Of all the spiritual mysteries, one that has consistently fascinated and perplexed people is the existence of otherworldly beings. The question always posed is: Are they real or myth? What does *your* heart see: myth or reality? I can answer absolutely that they are real. I use the term *being*, although *energy* may be more appropriate. These beings take on various identities dependent on the culture and the underlying spiritual/religious tradition that claim them. To one tradition, the beings may be called *angels*, whereas to another, their identity would be *god* or *goddess*. In reality, they are each unique and intrinsic sentient beings. It is a fascinating subject to explore, simple on the surface but very complex underneath.

The Norse gods and goddesses are real. The catch is to be able to determine from oral and written sources which are real; which may be elemental, natural forces, and/or powers such as fire; and which ones may be poetic license to teach hidden truths.

⚜

I don't believe in otherworldly beings. I know otherworldly beings. "If you are blind and have never seen the sun rise, it doesn't matter how many hypotheses you can array; you still don't know. Belief is simply the adoption of someone else's idea. Once you have seen the sun, you don't believe in it; you know it."[29]

I have been in the presence of otherworldly beings, which my wife identified as angels, but they just as well could have been identified as gods or goddesses. No matter what identity is assigned, most importantly, I have not seen angels in my mind, in a cloud formation, or in my dreams or as some type of human figure. I've been in the presence of and witness to an archangel and two assisting angels.

Having been in their presence, I know angels in the same way that I know a sunrise, the buzz of a bee, or rain falling on my head. I know otherworldly beings not with my mind but with my senses—no filters. It was a sensory first-hand experience.

Traditionally, the north is the symbolic realm of heavenly beings, including the ancestral spirits. I know this is correct, as the archangel and the two assisting angels appeared in the north, as traditionally recorded. It is important to keep in mind that all things of creation are unique and have a precise, intrinsic quality and identity.

The term *angel* is used within a certain philosophical tradition. Depending on the culture influenced by environment, oral tradition, and geographic location, the word could just as well be *god* or *goddess* to identify unseen energetic beings. The important knowledge is: unseen beings of the heavens and earth exist. In addition to the visitation, I have experienced earthly unseen beings known in Iceland as *huldufólk*, the hidden people or, as I call them, the hidden ones. I don't believe. I don't have faith. I know.

The term I use for this unprecedented event is *the Visitation*, which was witnessed by my wife, Sherry, and twelve of our apprentices. It occurred on the night of the new moon, Sunday, August 3, 1997, in the woods of Maine. I was also born on a new moon. Numerically, the date of the Visitation is a 10. The number 1 symbolizes the Absolute, the One, the Divine, the Great Mystery, the Creator. The number 10 symbolizes the reflection of the Divine or the perfection of creation. "In the number 10, creation reaches perfection and fulfillment. The masculine-positive, creative principle of God has penetrated and fertilized space, the negative, maternal aspect, and has become one with it."[30] In the Jewish tradition, the tenth letter of the alphabet is *Yod*. "*Yod* is the very first flame of the divine fire, of the spirit of God."[31] In the Jewish esoteric system of Kabbalah, "the tenth *sefirah*[32] is *Malkhuth*[33] and means kingdom."[34] And in the original tarot, the tenth card is the Wheel of Fortune. This is a card of choice, when we will continue to maintain our dualistic consciousness or let go of it and begin the journey to awaken to a consciousness of radical nonduality, when we shift our focus from materialism to one of spirit.

⚜

Otherworldly beings are awesome, essential, and most assuredly significant heavenly beings of creation who exist in a state of timelessness, not linear time. But since timelessness and linear time interpenetrate, they may appear anytime and are as close as a breath of air. But for them to physically appear and step into the stream of linear time and our reality, a purification of the elements that compose linear time must occur. Early on that Sunday afternoon, we experienced an otherworldly storm. One moment, the sky was crystal clear, tinged only with a few clouds, and in the next moment, the sky darkened into an ominous, swirling bluish-black tempest. There was a moment as if the world paused—there was no sound or movement as if a *jötunn* (giant) was holding its breath. And then…thunder, lightning, and rain—Þórr's pressence. Torrents of rain fell as thunder boomed overhead and lightning struck all around my wife, me, and our twelve apprentices.

At the time, we didn't know what to make of such an unusual natural occurrence. Approximately eight hours later, with the appearance of an archangel and two assisting angels as three immense pillars of light, the reason for the storm became apparent. The volume and intensity of the thunder and rain and the strength and force of the lightning was a purification of the earth and its elements. A major sanctification had taken place.[35]

At the Visitation, as messengers of the divine and in answer to my prayer, the archangel and the two assisting angels announced who I was in my previous incarnation through their presence and the other signs that were shown along with their appearance. "In biblical accounts, angels traditionally appeared in order to make an annunciation or a revelation of transcendent import. Usually an angel's message is one of concern not only to the individual who sees the vision, but to the collective group as well. Such visionary experiences mark dramatic turning points personally and culturally."[36] In the case of our twelve apprentices, my wife, and me, the Visitation was not a visionary experience but an actual physical, sensory, extraordinary event.

The Effect of the Visitation on Spiritual/ Philosophical/Religious Knowledge

During the Visitation, we experienced something that few humans believe in and even fewer get the experience to know. The majority of humanity's spiritual/philosophical/religious beliefs are based on secondhand knowledge, either written or oral, from others who have also based their beliefs on secondhand, thirdhand, and further removed knowledge.

This miraculous happening opened the gateway to knowing certain truths concerning spiritual/philosophical/religious beliefs. I will attempt to lay them out as best as I can. One further note, I believe that the Visitation provides Occam's razor validation for some aspects of physicist David Bohn's theories:

❖ **Knowledge: The interconnection and interpenetration of consciousness throughout the seen and unseen universe**.
David Bohm theorized a new reality of the universe. He named this reality the implicate order—the "hidden" aspect of the universe. "The theory of the implicate order contains an ultraholistic cosmic view; it connects everything with everything else. In principle, any individual element could reveal 'detailed information about every other element in the universe.' The central underlying theme of Bohm's theory is the 'unbroken wholeness of the totality of existence as an undivided, flowing movement without borders.'"[37] In other words, "Within the

implicate order, everything is connected; and, in theory, any individual element could reveal information about every other element in the universe."[38] Bohm named the known or visible universe or manifest world the "explicate order." In the implicate order, "'everything is enfolded into everything.' This is in contrast to the explicate order where things are unfolded."[39]

The Visitation provides proof of Bohm's theory as the physical appearance of the angels (immense pillars of light) was due to my prayer. For the angels to respond while in the implicate order, they would have had to have received the information from myself in the explicate order.[40]

After the intense, unusual storm, they were present in the afternoon but hidden[41] while they were still in a layer of the implicate order. It was only in the evening that they became visible to us in the explicate order—in Bohm's terms, when they unfolded.

❖ **Knowledge: Reincarnation**.
Based on what I knew within my heart I prayed for a sign to be given of who I was in my last incarnation: "Let them see a sign knowing that I was _____." I mentioned the name, as people would recognize it today.

The angels responding to my prayer indicated that I was alive before in a different body, place, and time. I am no different than anyone else. If I have had a past life (lives), then everyone else has had past lives. This is proof, as far as we can take it, considering we are attempting to prove the unprovable mysteries of life and creation—that our lives on earth are not a one-shot deal with a result of Heaven, Hell, or oblivion waiting for us.

But it is an ongoing death and rebirth evolution of our soul—our Golden DNA or Divine Spark/Starlight.

❖ **Knowledge**:
Sentient beings that humanity has named angels, gods, goddesses, bodhisattvas, and so forth physically exist even though they are usually hidden from sight while they remain in Bohm's implicate order. This leads to a conclusion that other sentient beings exist, namely gods and goddesses and others, such as elves and faeries and, in Iceland, the

hidden ones. But once again, they are in the implicate order and hidden from our senses and sight.

The Exorcist Who Came to the Sacred Mountain to Find Me: One Concluding Point

The following is excerpted from *Tequila and Chocolate: A Guide to a New Consciousness—The Awakening of Our Divinity and Humanity*:

As the time approached midnight, we were approaching a bridge over a small stream that led the way from one world to the next—one of prophetic sanctuary. This wooden bridge separated the rest of the cemetery from the realm and mausoleum of the Great One. (A warning to heed: never cross a bridge such as this without prayers and permission asked. This bridge was a gateway separating sacred space, and permission to enter must be granted.)

After crossing the bridge, we beheld the Lantern Hall in front of us, ablaze with hundreds of yellow-tinged specks of light, sparkling like bees of life and love. It was in front of this hall that the exorcist stopped and offered incense before he led us around the back to Kūkai's meditative residence. And it was here that the exorcism took place.

I believe there were approximately seven others, plus Keikō-san (our Japanese guide), the exorcist, and myself. He positioned us, except for Keikō-san, in a straight line facing Kōbō-Daishi's mausoleum and told us, through Keiko-san's translation, to sit still and relax. I was last in the line, with Keikō-san angled in front of and to the side, facing me.

He began working on each person, leaving me for last. He chanted, toned, and, every so often, screamed a spirit shout. Out of the corner of my eye, I could see him working rapidly with mudras, up and down each person's spine. The sounds coming out of the exorcist were eerily of another world and another time. Feeling as if I were in a dream, I closed my eyes. And in no time at all, I could feel the exorcist's presence and was unafraid.

The next part is hard, to say the least, to describe in words. I had a strong sensation of being disconnected yet connected at the same time. I was me but not me. I was the "I" in the "we" and the "we" in the "I," and felt like a top swirling in an every widening circle; and power, not the illusionary power of external humanness, but the power of Þórr, the bodhisattvas, the archangels, to put a name on it—power not of this earth, and I did not want to let go or return...but then...

A woman's scream penetrated the night and ripped through the very fabric of time...

I was back. Who am I? What am I? As my eyes slowly opened, the portals to my soul gazed upon the surreal scene before me. Keikō-san's face, beautiful as the dew glistening on a lily, was now frozen into a mask of terror. It had been her scream that had brought me back; on the other hand, had I ever left? This part of the cemetery contained a few stone lanterns. The shadows only heightened the mystical sense of wonder for me, as I felt incredibly powerful.

The visually shaken Keikō-san was stammering over her words to the exorcist. From a place of stillness, I silently watched the gestures and body language of the exorcist and Keikō-san, not knowing or caring about the words being exchanged. A moment ago—or was it an eternity ago?—I was in a space of power. But, no, I was the power. What did it all mean?

Keikō-san turned to face me and asked, "Are you all right? How do you feel?"

"I feel awesome and powerful. I can see so clearly, as if it is daylight...but mystified," I replied. "Was I transforming into one of the guardians who serve the Great One—the Daishi?"

"Well, yes...but no. You may look at it as a merging or interpenetration of energies, energies that few humans can accept much less survive. It is the first quickening of your *bodhicitta*—your divinity. The others who were here will deny what happened, out of fear and envy. We sent them back to the temple," said Keikō-san.

She then explained to me that the descending-spirit exorcism was a way to discover a spiritually sensitive person. This is a spiritually evolved person able to tap into other realities. "He believes that you are the most sensitive person he has ever worked with or met. This is why he came to Kōyasan—to find you. He had a dream of you," she explained. "But I had to stop him because I could see that you were not yourself."

❧

This abbreviated story hopefully fully illustrates my otherworldly experience—an experience that thrust me through a tear in the fabric of dualistic reality. Even the setting for the happening was mythically mystical. Commonly, exorcism is known as a spirit being taken off or out of a person who is supposedly possessed. A descending-spirit exorcism is where spirit merges or blends, interpenetrates, with a person. As recorded in the Bible, this was an experience of Jesus with the descent of spirit in the form of a dove.

As I looked back on my experience, the exorcism was the initial quickening of my awakening mind and a knowing of radical nondualistic interpenetrating reality. It was a sacred midnight happening I will never forget. The exorcism was performed by a Japanese esoteric, or shamanic, priest in October of 1987. It occurred in front of Kōbō Daishi's mausoleum on the sacred mountain Kōyasan. Kōbō Daishi was the founder of Shingon esoteric Buddhism. He is believed to be in eternal meditation in his mausoleum, awaiting the arrival of the next Buddha, Miroku Bosatsu.

❧

"I always remember your sensitive, strong, sacred spirit. It was a great experience for me too." Keikō-san, October, 1987

❧

❖ **Knowledge**:
   Reality is interpenetrative radical nonduality. I have experienced and have a knowing of this reality. In other words, reality is the blending and oneness of the absolute and relative, the spirit/divine and matter. We are in the divine, and the divine is within us.

What Follows

I am a mere human with unique intrinsic qualities and abilities. Within my humanness, I have a divine spark—starlight. I am divine and human. I have physically experienced and know through my senses the otherworld as much as any human may possibly know. Still, I make mistakes and am not perfect, or, as I like to teach, we are all perfect in our imperfections, which makes us perfect.

I've experienced the Nordic people, and their fjords, mountains, streams, and fields. Even though I was born in the United States, I have a Northern European Scottish Norse bloodline, which originated from Norwegian Norse settlers on the Scottish Hebrides and the Vikings of Normandy.

I believe the Norse sagas and eddas contain primordial knowledge, or what I call "first knowledge." However, to discover and decipher it is difficult. In discovering primordial knowledge, I utilize my physical experience of the otherworld, spiritual/shamanic knowledge, and physical rites and ceremonies of indigenous lineages passed on to my wife and me. I view written sources, scholarly or otherwise, not as an observer but as a practitioner of the knowledge. What follows is my best attempt to do so on my quest for knowledge and wisdom. I do this for the betterment of humanity, future generations, and the earth and all of its creatures.

CHAPTER 2

Norse Mythology

A myth is "a connecting link between scientific knowledge and emotional understanding. Myth, because it is not simply aligned with intellect, can never be entirely clear, but must also correspond to a nondualist metaphysics, in other words, a philosophy that is not purely rational and discursive."[42] Myth originates from the Greek word *mythos* which has a range of meanings such as word, story, and message.

But most importantly, myths are our magic mirror into the lives and ways of peoples past. These legendary tales give us a glimpse into their hopes, their fears, and their imaginations. Myths transcend time and space by revealing to us universal themes and life lessons that never become outdated. They are openings to the past that help us make sense of the world around us. The old tales continuously ring true within our hearts. If we choose to look, the lessons are always there. Order evolves out of chaos; there is death and rebirth, ritual and sacrifice, a journey to the underworld and the return of the sun and the birth of the hero twins, dragons and the slayers of monsters, and in most cultures, the heroic quest, the cup or bowl of plenty, and the sacred waters of the well or stream. These are just a few of the many different mythic themes that we may look to for knowledge and guidance throughout our life.

According to Joseph Campbell in *The Power of Myth*, there are two mythic orders. The first one concerns us as natural creatures. We are a part of the whole of nature. The second is "strictly sociological, linking you to a particular society. You are not simply a natural man, you are a member of a particular group."[43] Such as the Norse-Germanic cultural group. According to Campbell, "Every mythology has to do with the wisdom of life as related to a specific culture at a specific time. It integrates the individual into his society and the society into the field of nature. It unites the field of nature with my nature. It's a harmonizing force."[44]

Moreover, "The ancient tribes and cultures that are the ancestors of contemporary cultures and civilization created myth to help explain the natural world and humans' place in nature. It is interesting to note that a great many mythologies have a tree or column or mountain at the center of the world. The Scandinavians' identification with a great tree reflects their geographical location within the boreal forests of Northern Europe."[45]

⚜

Myths take many forms, just as there are many faces of Óðinn. Certain myths may present us with a glimpse of the Otherworld, its mysteries and truths. These mysteries of the unseen world are not explainable by left-brain, scientific thinking and belief or by dogmatic faith. The majority of people do not understand that the Bible is more mythical in context than literal. This is a tragedy, as the Bible being taken literally has caused and still causes death, destruction, and suffering. For the Christian faithful, it reinforces an "us versus them" mentality.

Contrary to this, the Norse-Germanic folk, as well as other pagan/heathen people, saw life more mystical than literal—with no sacred texts to soften their minds. What would have been supernatural to the Christians was natural to the Norse. Nature was their guide, the sky above and the earth below. They tapped into the power of their ancestors and the unseen world. They worshipped in nature and respected the power of the sky, the sea, and the earth. Lightning was not only a physical occurrence but was Þórr's hammer, announcing his presence. Two ravens sitting together were just that—two birds together, but were also a sign of Óðinn's presence.

Nature is one of the means for us to be able to see life through a mythical consciousness rather than a literal one. We develop a natural consciousness and a strong mind and heart the closer we are to nature. It is here where we feel and experience oneness, not a separation from all things of the earth.

Many cultures have a primary myth of a dying and resurrected god/goddess—a death and rebirth deity. Christianity is not the sole bearer of this mythic motif. Other cultures have their own resurrected deities, to name a few: Tammuz, Quetzalcoatl, Adonis, Osiris, Inanna, Persephone, Baldr, and of course

Óðinn. The myths of these deities point us in one direction—primordial knowledge. The knowledge revealed to us in these myths is the immortality of our soul and the truth of reincarnation. I know this truth. It is not based on belief or faith but on wisdom—my knowing through physical experience.

Myths are rooted in truth and provide us with spiritual/religious teachings, some obvious and some hidden. They may contain moral and ethical guidance. I believe primordial knowledge is right in front of our faces in the Norse-Germanic myths, especially the ones surrounding Óðinn, Þórr, and Freyja. In conclusion, myths allow us to have our own hero's journey. Our journey, difficult though it my be, is to return a green philosophy to humanity and the earth. This is our hero's journey.

Hyperborea

Where my primordial soul knowledge originated was at first a mystery to me. As time has progressed this lifetime, I have come to the conclusion that the roots of it flow from the surviving knowledge of one or more ancient civilizations—ones recognizable as past golden ages. I am not alone in this belief. According to Elsa-Brita Titchenell:

> The Norse eddas contain science and philosophy of a high order, a rounded knowledge, which also constituted religion to some long-forgotten people who must have preceded the Viking age by no one knows how long. Judging by the thoughts they incorporated in their tales, they included in their world picture an awareness of many of the forces and potencies we know by different names and which have been rediscovered by science during the past century or so. Considering that the Norse tradition, though dating back in essentials to an unknown prehistory, has had to pass through the rough-and-tumble world of the Viking warriors and has no doubt had to draw on a more vivid palette in depicting the adventures of gods and giants than originally used, it is remarkable how much profound philosophy is recognizable to us today.[46]

To further my personal seeking, I led a small group of adventurers to Scotland and the Orkney Islands in the fall of 2011. Around the same time, drillers looking for oil under the North Sea discovered something very interesting. They found traces of an ancient land with hills, valleys, and rivers. It is estimated the land was swallowed by the sea some 8500 years ago. This lost land may date as far back as 18,000 BCE. It was the heartland of Europe for humanity. Could this have been the legendary Hyperborea?

I believe so as "somewhere near the icy regions of the North Pole, legend speaks of an ancient and mostly forgotten civilization. Mythical in character, the Hyperborean civilization is said to have flourished in the northern most region of planet Earth at a time when the area was suitable for human habitation."[47] According to certain esoteric systems and spiritual traditions, Hyperborea was the terrestrial and celestial beginning of civilization. Some theories postulate Hyperborea was the original Garden of Eden, the point where the earthly and heavenly planes interpenetrated. And it is said that humans transgressed divine law in this golden age with the ultimate price being banishment to the outside world. Humans ventured into other regions of Earth, establishing new civilizations, thus bringing to an end this great and glorious golden age.

The ancient Greeks referred to Hyperborea as a land of perpetual sun beyond the North Wind where their god Apollo spent part of his time primarily during the winter. It was a land of plenty, free of toil, where its enlightened inhabitants lived beyond a normal lifespan. This was the land of the blessed. No wonder the sacred sites of Delos and Delphi were connected with this primordial paradise at the top of the world.

This mythic land may be the origination of the concept of a primordial tradition. As Hyperborea sank beneath the waves, this primordial knowledge spread throughout the earth and may be discovered within various traditions. I believe this esoteric knowledge is to be discovered within ancient Egypt, the hidden teachings of Moses, Hinduism, esoteric Buddhism, ancient Greece, and of course, the Germanic-Norse Tradition. It is interesting to note that an enlightened society located in the far north corresponds nicely with the symbolism of the pole and the concept of the world tree positioned on a north-south axis.

Yggdrasill—World Tree/Tree of Life/Tree of Knowledge

The world tree is a mythic motif found in all indigenous cultures. In these cultures, the wise ones, sometimes referred to as shamans, looked to the earth and then to the sky and saw the connection between the two—trees. They are one of humankind's most powerful symbols. Trees represent fertility, immortality, and the totality of life as well as being a link between heaven and earth. Rooted firmly and deeply in the earth, trees reach up to the heavens and provide an appropriate mythical symbology for a central link between the seen and unseen worlds.

> Trees are symbols of interconnection. Since a tree grows from earth down into the underworld and up into the heavens, it connects the three worlds. It represents "as above, so below" (as in Heaven, so on Earth) and "as below, so above" (as in the underworld, so on earth).[48] The tree is also a symbol of the embodiment of the macrocosm in the microcosm, of the transpersonal, of the transpersonal embodied in the personal, for each tree has a unique, individual shape, yet manifests a universal pattern of growth and development by which the four elements (soil, water, air, and light) are incorporated into its substance.[49]

The shamans had the ability to connect the profane to the sacred, thus providing a link between heaven (the otherworld) and earth. At various times, I use the word *heaven* not in a Christian context or Neo-shamanic context of an upper world but as meaning the unseen realms of the universe—the otherworld.

The wise ones of the past accessed the otherworld through a shift in consciousness. Many times, this involves a form of trance where we journey to the otherworld. This trance state may be brought about through various modalities, such as extreme temperatures or through the ingestion of hallucinogenic plants and substances. In other words, these wise ones access the unseen spiritual realms while still in the physical realm. One of the key factors of a shaman's proficiency is his or her level of sensitivity, to be open and aware of the intertwining forces of heaven and earth, and the ability to access both for knowledge and wisdom. The most advanced shamans are so sensitive and open to the oneness of both realms that they could access the otherworld at any time, without relying on outside tools.

Mythically, the means of journeying was often depicted as a horse, such as Óðinn's horse, Sleipnir. In Old Norse, *Sleipnir* means "slipper, sliding one," indicting Óðinn's ability to slip or slide through the eight directions of the seen and unseen worlds. Eight is the number of infinity.

Journeys, whether they are spiritual or physical, need a road map, a path, landmarks, and especially, a destination. Our journey seeking a green philosophy, command of ourselves, and primordial knowledge is no different. We need a symbolic connection to the otherworld. A tree is the perfect symbol—a metaphoric tree of the world, the mythological world tree.

Since the world tree is a central axis mundi connecting various numbers of worlds, it becomes the primordial road map and allows the shaman access to other worlds and realms while metaphorically providing a central point of balance and harmony. Many traditional cultures, such as the Celtic, considered trees to be sacred, mystical, and impregnated with a divine creative energy. To the Celtic, Norse, and other European people, the oak, ash, and yew were considered sacred.

The Norse-Germanic world tree has two candidates for its identity—Irminsul and Yggdrasill. The mythological Germanic holy tree Irminsul qualifies as a symbolic world tree as it is identified as a gigantic pillar. Symbolically, pillars connect heaven and earth. Thus, Irminsul would be the world pillar or universal column.

Our other tree, Yggdrasill, may be identified as a tree of knowledge and tree of life. It also makes sense that Yggdrasill may be identified as a world tree. Irminsul and Yggdrasill may be one and the same. In seeking primordial knowledge, we will focus our attention on Yggdrasill as the tree of nine worlds and the tree of knowledge and life.

Most references classify Yggdrasill as an ash tree. On the other hand, Yggdrasill may have been a yew tree. In Old Norse, an alternative name for the yew was *barraskr*, needle ash. This has lead scholars to identify Yggdrasill as an ash tree. Common sense deems Yggdrasill's identity as an ash tree inaccurate, as it sheds its leaves in the winter. However, the yew has needles and is evergreen (a concept of immortality-eternity) and an appropriate symbol for a world tree/tree of life/tree of knowledge (the last designation an appropriate one as witnessed by Óðinn's sacrifice-seeking knowledge).

Additionally, the yew is one of the longest-living trees and bleeds a red-colored resin symbolizing blood. This magical tree is an appropriate symbol for life and sacrifice. Yggdrasill is the tree Óðinn hangs from for nine long nights in an act of self-sacrifice. "Yggdrasill denotes the 'steed of Óðhinn,' but it can also mean 'I-carrier'—the supporter of the conscious self. The oldest European names for the yew go back to the Germanic *iwe* (iwa), which is related to *ihhe* (ihha), the first-person singular. And in Anglo-Saxon *ih* means both 'I' (the conscious self) and the yew tree…Another Angelo-Saxon name of the yew tree, *eo*, stems from Old High German *eo*, also meaning 'eternal' and 'always.' Somehow, the yew tree has always reflected eternal consciousness."[50] This is the primordial knowledge of immortality—eternal consciousness.

The Bee and the Sacred Mead

In all philosophical traditions, the numbers three and nine (3 x 3) are sacred. The Norse embraced the magical properties of these numbers. We have the nine worlds, the three Norns, and the Elder Futhark runes. This runic alphabet is arranged in three groups of eight each for a total of twenty-four runes. Three is the divine number of power and prosperity. Interestingly enough in nature, there is an insect which exhibits an unusual occurrence of the number three—the bee, which is ruled, I might add, by a queen. "In three days, the egg of the queen is hatched. It is fed for nine days (3 x 3). It reaches maturity in fifteen days (5 x 3). The worker grub reaches maturity in twenty-one days (7 x 3). And is at work three days after leaving its cell. The drone matures in twenty-four days (8 x 3). The bee is composed of three sections—head and two stomachs. The two eyes are made up of about three thousand small eyes, each (like the cells of the comb) having six sides (2 x 3). Underneath the body are six (2 x 3) wax scales with which the comb is made. It has six (2 x 3) legs. Each leg is composed of three sections. The foot is formed of three triangular sections. The antennae consist of nine (3 x 3) sections. The sting has nine (3 x 3) barbs on each side."[51]

Worldwide, bees are acknowledged as being essential for human survival. Bees have been the sacred, soulful guide for humanity for time immemorial. They are messengers of love. Bees are thought to have survived since the last golden age. Their hum, sometimes referred to as the voice of the goddess, vibrates a song of sweetness and life that mirrors a paradise of innocence and love. The gift of the bees is honey, life, and mead.

Life is poetry in motion fueled by the sacredness of mead. This is the mead of poetry of the Norse. The making of the golden mead only resulted after the reconciliation of the previously warring gods and goddesses, the Aesir, and the earthly deities, the Vanir. To seal their peace, both groups spit into a cauldron. As a symbol of their reconciliation, they created a giant named Kvasir, divine wisdom, the wisest of all creatures. To limit the spread of this divine conscious-ness of wisdom, and to dominate this knowledge for themselves, two dwarves killed Kvasir and captured his blood. According to Snorri, to keep the blood safe it was put into "two vessels, Boðn and Són, and in a cauldron, Óðrœrir."[52]

The dwarves then mix Kvasir's blood with honey, resulting in the mead of poetry. The original name of the mead was Óðrœrir (Old Norse approximately "the one that stimulates to ecstasy").[53] Thus, Óðrœrir may refer to the vessel as well as the mead.

Eventually, "the three vessels pass into the possession of the giant Suttungr, and it is from him that Odin finally steals the mead."[54] It is through his sha-manic shape-shifting ability and his mercurial thievery that Óðinn was able to abscond with the vats of poetic mead. As a final note, honey is bee spit.

Tree of Life and Tree of Knowledge

> Beloved, gaze in thine own heart, the
> holy tree is blooming there.
> —W. B. YEATS, "TWO TREES"

There are two primary trees recorded within the Norse-Germanic tradition—Irminsul and Yggdrasill—and one not as well-known—Mímameiðr, Mimir's tree. In Genesis, there are two primary named trees—the Tree of Knowledge and the Tree of Life. The Tree of Knowledge is dogmatically referred to as the Tree of Knowledge of Good and Evil—a dualistic concept that over the mil-lennia has caused untold suffering. Christianity used this weapon in their attempted destruction and conversion of the pagans by identifying the Norse-Germanic gods and goddesses as evil.

Translations of oral and written knowledge and languages may always be manipulated. This is the case in identifying the Tree of Knowledge as being the Tree of Good and Evil. The truer translation of the ancient Hebrew is "pure and impure." This is a great shift in meaning from a mind-set of good and evil to pure and impure. Additionally, even though they are portrayed as two sepa-rate trees, the Tree of Life and the Tree of Knowledge, they are one and the same. If this is the hidden knowledge of Genesis, what about the Norse?

As there was no word for *evil* in Old Norse, which meant morally repre-
hensible or sinful, Yggdrasill could not be identified in terms of good and evil.
However, the essence of Yggdrasill seems to point to it being pure and impure,
not good and evil. Yggdrasill is a divine tree. This means it is pure. Is it solely
pure? Or is there a quality of impurity about it? The dragon Nidhogg gnaws
at the roots of Yggdrasill, indicating a state of impurity through destructive
forces.

Knowledge concerning Nidhogg comes from various sources. In Old
Norse, the name means "the one striking full of hatred."[55] This corresponds to
an impure state of mind. According to the *Dictionary of Northern Mythology*,
Nidhogg "is a dragon of death in Voluspa which drinks the blood of the dead
and eats corpses. *Voluspa 66* describes how it will live in Nidavellir in the new
world after the Ragnarok. In Grimnismal 32 and 35, it lives under and gnaws
at the roots of the world ash Yggdrasill. A squirrel, Ratataoskr, is a go-between
messenger between Nidhogg and the eagle who sits in the branches of the
ash bringing discord. Snorri repeats this information from Grimnismal in
Gylfaginning 14 and 15, while in Gylfaginning 51, he repeats the passage from
Voluspa 39 in a different form in which Nidhogg torments the dead in the
spring Hvergelmir and thus becomes like the dragon in Christian visionary literature, with elements of hell-like places of punishment."[56]

Symbolically, the true nature of Yggdrasill could be comparable to the
concept of the lotus flower, which opens to the light (pure) but lives in the
mud (impure). For us, our impurity does not come from states of physical or
dogmatic religious uncleanliness but from states of mind destructive to our
soul, such as greed, doubt, fear, and anger—the anger that turns to wrath and
revenge such as in a blood feud.

Metaphysically, we are dealing not only with a macrocosmic concept but
a reflection of microcosmic principles, which lie within all human beings. The
two trees depicted in Genesis are one and the same, the Tree of Knowledge
and the Tree of Life, both of which are macrocosmic and microcosmic in form.
They are not only eternal to us but are internal—within us, as our spinal column. Physically and spiritually, our spinal tree, Yggdrasill—our internal tree of
knowledge (divineness) and life (humanness)—carries the messages from its
earthly roots, our hips, legs, and feet,[57] up to our heavenly connection, specifically the pineal and pituitary glands seated within our brain. In other words,

each of us carries within us a micro Yggdrasill and its nine worlds. We may even expand Yggdrasill's symbolic aspects to correspond with our human body, where the eagle at the top of the tree represents our brain as well as the power of our spirit.

Children of Ash

The Hebrew story of the origination of humans begins with Adam, the male, being formed from the ground out of clay, possibly red earth. The utilization of clay probably originates with the Egyptians and their potter god Khnum, who created the first children on his potter's wheel with clay from the banks of the Nile. However, in the Christian version, Adam is formed out of dust with the female, Eve, is birthed from the rib of Adam.

According to the Norse, and in contrast to this Christian silliness, we have the first human male and female as two separate pieces of driftwood. Óðinn and his brothers, Vili and Vé, are walking on the seashore and come upon two pieces of driftwood. With their divine sight, they observe "forms" within the driftwood and release them (Askr – ash-tree and Embla). This is the same mythological methodology where the cosmic cow Auðhumbla, licked the salty blocks of ice, releasing the forms within the ice.

Instead of Adam and Eve, we have Askr (male) and Embla (female). Driftwood is a fascinating symbol. It comes from the sea; lands on the shore by the action of waves, tides, and/or winds; and its intrinsic shapes are then formed by the fire of the sun and the winds of the sky. Just as each of us is intrinsically different, so is driftwood. Nature forming humanity is consistent with the evolutionary theory of earthly creation.

What then is the message out of these two different symbolic approaches to the birthing of humanity? Within the Christian myth,[58] the female is birthed from the male, a not so subtle indication of the superiority of men over women. No equality of sexes in that tale. Additionally, clay or dust is solely of the earth, while trees have their roots in the ground but extend upward to the heavens. Trees are of both heaven and earth. Trees are majestic. The message from the Norse mythology is a teaching of soul importance—each of us, just like the trees, is intrinsically magnificent and needs to reach for the heavens, to ascend as the eagle to the light of enlightenment and know that we are each a heavenly divine as well as an earthly human.

The Third Tree

In Norse mythology, there is a third mentioned tree—Mimir's tree, Mímameiðr. Mimir's tree is the Tree of Knowledge. Scholars have theorized that it is another name for Yggdrasill. We discover some interesting things about Mímameiðr. One bit of hidden knowledge is the depiction of the golden rooster Víðópnir, who sits on the highest bough of Mímameiðr. Roosters welcome the dawn. Microcosmically, this translates to our own personal awakening. When our rooster crows, our spark awakens and our Tree of Knowledge of Duality transforms into our Tree of Life of Oneness. Let your rooster crow!

CHAPTER 3

Creation and the Nine Worlds

The Norse creation myth is similar to other cultures, as it originates within a void. The Norse used the term *Ginnungagap* for this emptiness. It was only after the marriage of fire and ice that creation appeared. Muspelheim, the realm of pure fire, is located in the south. Across the abyss, in the north, lies the icy realm of Niflheim. The heat and fiery sparks thrown off melted the ice, and from this interaction of fire and ice, a giant, Ymir, was born. It was then that Óðinn and his two brothers carved up the giant, which created the known universe. This is the commonly accepted translation. Could there be a deeper meaning from a hidden or different translation? Scandinavian researcher, religious historian, and author Maria Kvilhaug believes so.

The first two lines of stanza three in "Völuspá" of the *Poetic Edda* are generally translated as, and I paraphrase, "In the beginning of Ages (Of old was the Age)...the hot and cold streams birthed a giant—Ymir (when Ymir lived)." Kvilhaug explains the translation as, "In the Beginning was the Wave; when Sound was building."[59]

Another way to put this is "as the hour approaches for the birth of a cosmos, the heat from Muspelheim (home of fire) melts the ice massed in Niflheim (cloud home), creating fertile vapor in the Void. This is Ymir, the frost giant, from which the gods will create worlds: unmanifest worlds and 'victory worlds,' wherein the rivers of lives will embody."[60] I refer to this particular stage of the myth as the "Great Silence."[61] Furthermore, "Ymir is sustained by the four streams of milk flowing in the four directions from the cow Audhumla, symbol of fertility, the still unmanifest seed of life. 'Slain' by the gods, Ymir becomes Orgalmer (primal loud noise), the keynote whose overtones vibrate throughout the sleeping shelves of space. Like the Tibetan Fohat which sets the atoms spinning, this graphically describes a first vibration organizing motion in inert protosubstance, creating vortices whose amplitudes and velocities determine the wavelengths and frequencies that make the various ranges of matter."[62]

⚜

The concept of fire and ice interpenetrating to birth creation has a deeper meaning than the interaction of fire and water as metaphors for the blending of the absolute principle with the relative principle. If we consider our divine spark (Óðinn's seed) within us as being encased in ice, it will take the fire of our spirit to melt the ice and release or awaken our seed of immortality. This divine energy, that lies unawakened in the majority of people, when awakened, will at times feel like an icy fire flowing within the physical body. I know this as I have experienced it many times. This feeling could be described as an ecstatic state of being, which is one of the hallmarks of the shaman and shamanism.

⚜

Since "the religion of the ancient Norseman is one of the most difficult to describe, indeed far more so than are the older religions of Rome, Greece, Egypt, Israel, Persia, or India,"[63] scholars differ in their opinions about the mythic geography of the nine worlds. According to Ralph Metzner in *The Well of the Remembrance*, Yggdrasill "symbolizes and constitutes the common axis on which the nine worlds, or realms of existence, are arranged. There are five worlds on the central axis—one in the center, two above, and two below—and four more in the four directions at the central plane."[64]

In the Middle World, we have Muspelheim (Realm of Fire and Heat) in the south and Niflheim (Realm of Ice and Cold) in the north. In the west is Vanaheim. This is the land of the Vanir, the gods and goddesses of the earth. Opposite it in the east is Jotunheim—the home of the giants. It is easy to label the giants/giantesses as evil ones, but order and chaos may be a better identity. In reality, they are the primal powers of the universe. It makes sense the giants/giantesses, a.k.a. powers, are situated in the east.

Finally, Midgard, the Middle Garden, completes the realms of the Middle World. It is located in the center of the four directions. It lies on the central axis of the world tree. This would equate with earth—humans, animals, fish, birds, mountains, rivers, oceans, and so forth. It's interesting to note "*Gard* means 'dwelling' and is related to 'garden.'"[65] Could this identity come from Hyperborea just as the mythology of the Garden of Eden possibly came from the same source?

Below, Midgard on the central axis is Svartalfheim. It is the realm of the Dwarves or the Black Elves. This is the first level of the Lower World. Directly below Svartalfheim is Hel or the Land of the Dead, which is different from heavenly Valhöll—warriors paradise. Hel is the home of the Death Goddess. This lower world of the dead is not the hell of Christian dogma. It is not a place of eternal damnation.

In the upper world, on the central axis right above Midgard, is Ljossalheim. This is the realm of the light elves and the air spirits. Above the light elves, on the central axis, is Asgard, home of the Aesir (gods and goddesses). "Originally, Asgard was probably understood to be part of Midgard, which meant that the gods lived close to the world of men, as opposed to Utgard,[66] the area outside."[67] Snorri, however, locates Asgard in the sky or heavens, a definite influence of his Christian faith. In regards to our journey, locating Asgard close to the world of humans matches, to an extent, with the concept of no separation between the world of spirit and the world of matter. In this case, Asgard and Midgard interpenetrate. In Snorri's account, Asgard is connected to Midgard by the rainbow bridge, Bifrost. Rainbows are beautiful and an awesome sign of earthly and otherworldly power as rainbows are formed from the interpenetration of fire (sun) and water (rain). A native Hawaiian friend of mine says, "No rain, no rainbows!"

⚜

No matter the exact location of the worlds, Midgard (the seen) and the otherworlds (unseen) interpenetrate, forming a oneness of creation. The universe, the totality of Yggdrasill's essence (seen and unseen) and everything in it, is not dualistic in essence. The universe and all things have a quintessence of radical nonduality. This principle is revealed in Óðinn's other name: Allfather.

Over the previous earth ages, humanity has flowed from a golden age of equality to a matriarchal ruling paradigm and finally to a patriarchal one. Of course, there are transition times between the ages. Many times, these ages are represented by metals of the earth—gold, silver, copper, bronze, and iron.

The gender identity of the sun, that great life-giving force, helps identify the focus of the culture. In matriarchal cultures, the sun is feminine, a goddess, whereas in patriarchal societies, the sun is masculine, the god. Both views are unbalanced when utilized as dogma. The prevailing paradigm of the golden age, where primordial knowledge originated, was neither matriarchal nor patriarchal. Its prevailing religious belief was neither solar nor lunar; it was stellar—the reality and light behind the seen world.

A common view over time has been that the earth is feminine—Mother Nature. A few esoteric cultures have expanded that identity out to the stars as see the universe as Mother Nature. It doesn't take a lot of common sense to realize the earth as feminine is appropriate, as the earth and the sky nurture and nourish all things. Additionally, the universe as Mother Nature is a great concept for us to embrace. It expands our concern and consciousness for the well-being of all things out to the stars. This shift in consciousness and awareness is an important issue, now and in the future, as technology further allows the exploration and, quite possibly, the exploitation and military use of space.

In the case of the sun and moon, the sun (Sol) was feminine and a goddess in Norse mythology with the moon (Mani) being male, a god and brother to the sun. The Norse were not alone in this belief. Many other cultures held similar beliefs, such as Japanese Shintoism, where Amaterasu is the sun goddess and Tsukuyomi the moon god. For our seen world, identifying the sun and moon as a goddess or god is a choice, as long as it integrates with other beliefs. Understanding the mysteries of life through symbolism is important to our understanding of ourselves and others, not solely through the gender identity. One primary example: the sun symbolizes our hearts, while the moon symbolizes our minds. The moon has no light of its own, only what it receives from the sun. This means our heart knows truth while our mind only knows discursive knowledge—that which is obtained by reason and argument rather than intuition. "Intuitive thought is naked, unmediated apprehension, immediately given (to experience), whereas discursive thought is mediated and articulated instead within language. Intuition is noninferential awareness of abstract or concrete truths."[68]

The Three Wells

To discover the religious beliefs of the ancient Norse is very difficult. Even the simple location of the various worlds and the three wells is problematic, let alone deciphering their actual rituals and beliefs. For instance, some consider the location of some of the worlds as being by the wells that sustain the world tree. Yggdrasill has three roots nourished by three wells: Urd's well, Mimir's well, and Hvergelmir (Old Norse "bubbling cauldron"). The wells are under the roots of Yggdrasill. Tree roots grow into the ground, and from a human perspective, this would be the lower world. The earth we stand on would be the middle world, and the sky above the upper world. From this perspective, Hvergelmir (located in *Niflheim*) would be located in the lower world. This makes sense, as *Niflheim* in Old Norse means "the dark world." Following this logic, Urd's well and Mimir's well would also be found in the lower world, under the roots of the world tree. However, according to other scholars, the three wells are located vertically, in each of the three primary worlds: Urd is placed in the upper world, Mimir's well is on the earth plane, and Hvergelmir is located in Niflheim, in the lower world. Keep in mind, there is no upper, middle, or lower world, only this world, the seen universe, and the otherworld, the unseen universe. The use of the terms *upper*, *middle*, and *lower* is only a tool to help us get our heads around the concept of the unseen world, the otherworld that interpenetrates our world.

Considering primordial knowledge, all three wells located in the lower world is more plausible than a well in each level. It also makes more sense if we consider the lower world, as the oldest world and the foundation of everything. Accordingly, "all three roots of Yggdrasill and the three wells that nourish them are located in the lower world, the oldest part of the universe. The three wells are arranged horizontally along a north-south line. Hvergelmir lies in the north, Mimir's well in the center, directly beneath the trunk of Yggdrasill, and Urd's well to the south."[69]

If we view this knowledge from a radical nondualistic perspective, locating the three wells in the lower world would make sense, whereas, from a human perspective, the relative term *dark* is the origin of all things (all matter). Going one step further with radical nonduality, the three vertical realms of existence I've discussed are, in reality, one realm, where the three interpenetrate, and the relative/absolute light (spirit) interpenetrates the dark (matter).

Where is the truth? I do not believe in dogma or doctrine. This book is a book of wisdom. This means you take any information and knowledge within these pages, add your experience of life, spiritual practice and common sense, and determine what your truth is and what will help you awaken from materialistic sleep, educate others about green philosophy, and become a better divine human being—an expression of the energy of Óðinn.

Aesir and Vanir

It is generally accepted in mythology that there are two classifications of gods and goddesses, heavenly and earthly. Generally, if a culture is matriarchal, the deities are of the earth, whereas in patriarchal societies, they are more frequently considered heavenly. The Aesir were the sky gods of the Norse and the Vanir were the land and sea deities. Óðinn, Baldr, Þórr, Tyr, Loki, Frigg, and Idunn, to name a few, were the Aesir. The Vanir were gods and goddesses of the earth, such as Freyja; her brother, Freyr; and Njörðr.

According to the eddas, and possibly in an attempt to understand the tension and conflict between two conflicting philosophies—such as a patriarchal culture in opposition to a matriarchal one—the Aesir and Vanir warred. But in their eventual reconciliation, the Mead of Poetry was created.

Even though the eddas portray a separation on one hand between the Aesir and Vanir, primordial knowledge would indicate the unity of deities of both heaven and earth. Primarily all the Norse-Germanic gods and goddesses were called Aesir. Additionally, Freyja "lives in heaven at a place called Folkvangr, and when she moves into battle, she gets half of the fallen warriors, Odin receiving the other half."[70] It seems Old Norse mythology assimilated various Vanir into the hierarchy of the Aesir, as Freyja is both of the heavens and the earth. Could this come from older knowledge, where the earthly Freyja and the heavenly Frigg are one and the same?

Keep in mind, Óðinn's wisdom (spirit) is intimately connected with all aspects of the earth, its forces, and the joys and struggles of life—Þórr, son of the earth (life struggles), is also the son of Óðinn. Wisdom comes from the experience of knowledge (mind). It is important that this experience comes from the earth/nature and is experienced through our bodies (heart) where our body/mind is one.

When the Gods Battle Once Again

The end times—these three simple words cause fear and terror in the minds of many people, as they open a portal to dogmatic manipulation based on interpretations of the last book of the Bible, Revelations. Ironically enough, we are in the end times, but not in the way that the religious manipulators want you to believe.

The end times means, simply, the end of an age—the Age of Pisces. As a human race, we are in a transition period between the Age of Pisces and the beginning of the Age of Aquarius—this is the foretold next golden age. Hyperborea could possibly have been the earth's last golden age. At that time, the earth seems to have been a garden paradise where love and equality reigned supreme. Institutional hierarchy was unknown. There was only natural law and the spirit of egalitarianism, and divine wisdom flowed freely.

Over the past thirty years, I have been privy to various indigenous prophecies concerning earth changes. They are all similar and don't paint a pretty picture of humanity's future. The elders all said that man must stop destroying the earth through their greed and need for power.

One of these elders was Vince Stogan, a Salish Indian doctor. He didn't call himself a shaman, but if you needed a label, he preferred to be called an Indian doctor. However, he did refer to his uncle, alive during the early part of the twentieth century, as a shaman. In fact, a "strong shaman" was his term as in "strong heart, strong mind, and strong hands for healing." Vince told my wife and me about the prophecies of his uncle:

My uncle predicted all the events that would happen, and they all have been or come true (bombs, World War II, TV, cars, styles, etc.). If things don't calm down over in the Middle East, it will be another war that will be big, World War III—a part of the earth will change. Uncle said it would be like a little boy picking on another little boy; then, one of their big brothers will join in, and then another member, until the whole family is fighting, and it will spread to everybody joining in and choosing sides.

⚜

Ragnarok is the Nordic end times—the final destiny of the gods. Vince's uncle's prophecy is similar in tone to stanza 45 of "Voluspa" (Prophecy of the Volva), the best-known poem of the *Poetic Edda*:

> Brothers will fight their own brothers
> And be their kin's slayers
> Children of sisters will
> Betray their relations:
> Hardness is in the world,
> Prostitution abounds,
> Axe age, sword age
> Shields are cleft asunder
> Wind (death) age, wolf (greed) age
> Before all the world plunges
> No man will
> Spare another.[71]

Once again, we witness the potential fate of humanity. As with Revelations, Ragnarok can be difficult to decipher. Within the myth of Ragnarok (or is it a warning?), we must be careful of our understanding and interpretation of oral legends in written form.

The New Age

I believe the oral traditions of Ragnarok may be based on the experience of volcanic eruptions as well as a much older teaching and warning that preceded the Viking Age. The teaching is a diagram or road map for transformation and awakening through overcoming such things as greed and fear. The field of battle is not outside us but within.

It also forewarns and reminds humanity of the cyclical nature of reality, the birthing and passing of ages, and humanity's partnership in the workings of creation—cosmic change and transformation. Gods battle against chaotic forces, the forces of the underworld, with the end result being that from destruction, the world is birthed anew (again, death and rebirth/resurrection).

Interestingly enough, three of the gods who survive are Baldr, spirit and the light of courage; his blind brother Hodr, who kills Baldr; and their half brother, Vali, the avenger who slays Hodr.

The mythic aspects of Baldr's murder are very interesting and revealing. I won't delve into the full story, but I will point out that "Baldr represents human virtues that once were nurtured—the virtues of courage, objectivity, unprejudiced, kindness, and wisdom. These virtues were murdered by another human trait—ignorance, jealousy, and blind aggression."[72] In other words, our destructive darkness, our beast within, kills wisdom and the light of our spirit.

⚜

From the fires and floods of Ragnarok, a new age, a golden age, will be birthed. The Norse had a name for the golden age, "Fróðafriðr, which means the peace of wisdom,"[73]

This is the key that opens the gateway to the future. We all may become wise and peaceful while escaping the prison that organized religion and other destructive paradigms, such as capitalism, have put us in, using fear and greed to put a stranglehold on our minds. The key needed to open our prison is to be found after we have overcome and/or bound our destructive passions[74] through personal power and wisdom. A return to a green philosophy, along with the wisdom of Óðinn and the power of Þórr and Freyja's power of nature, will help us discover our keys and escape our self-imposed imprisonment while birthing our own inner golden age.

CHAPTER 4

Reality of the Otherworld

Many people approach the otherworld (spirit world) from a dualistic perspective. Usually, their consciousness pictures it as "up there somewhere." From a Christian dualistic standpoint, Heaven is up and Hell is down, and after physical death, you end up for eternity in one or the other. While alive, the only link you have to Heaven is through the Church and their priests/ministers. There is no direct spiritual link for the faithful. The Church is the gatekeeper.

Other dualistic paradigms view the otherworld as being behind a veil or metaphorically separated by a body of water, such as a river. I've even used these concepts in my writings in an attempt to explain the unexplainable. But what if the exact opposite is true, and there is no separation between us and the otherworld, no separation between spirit and matter? The Norse were closer to this truth, sometimes viewing the entrance to the otherworld as within a holy hill or mountain, and at other times, the entrance was to be found within a graveyard. The Icelandic Norse strongly believed, and they still believe, in the existence of the hidden people with their homes within the stones found on their island.

Furthermore, "as is sometimes the case in Icelandic folktales, the otherworld in *Grelent* and *Tidorel* seems to be in, or near, water and the characters even have to go into the water to penetrate into the other world."[75] This is exactly the case in the sacrificial self-to-self[76] rite of bathing, when a person enters a river, enabling them to access the otherworld. However, entering into a river does not unto itself provide access to the otherworld. It is the spirit song (*galdr*) sung at the beginning of the ritual by a person of power—a shaman, if you will—which "opens" the river and provides the access to the otherworld.

Shamanism

My knowledge of shamanism flows from my firsthand experience of it. I have not been an observer but an active participant, initiate, and carrier of shamanic lineages, ranging from my shamanic initiation in a sacred lagoon in the Andes after having walked the Inca Trail, to my wife and I apprenticing with Mom and Vince Stogan, Coast Salish shamans, who passed on to us their shamanic lineage of bathing, burning (blót), and healing. Our deeds of shamanic power have been witnessed and felt by others. Thus, I approach this subject not from an archeological or scholarly approach but from my direct experience of the subject matter. Vince once stated that I had the strongest healing hands that he had ever seen. Since there is always an imperfection to perfection, he also said I was impatient and too fast in healing. Patience is a trait I am continuously working on.

Traditionally, shamanism has been identified as a journey of the soul conducted by the shaman, known as a master of the spirits. A shaman is a person with the ability to connect the profane to the sacred, and thus provide a link between the otherworld and earth. He or she is a visionary and what I call a "pathfinder to the soul." Shamans are dreamers, philosophers, and undogmatic religious guides and teachers.

A shaman is also a person of power who dream-voyages to the otherworld for knowledge and freedom. This is the freedom from our ego-self, the unhealthy ego. The shaman helps others, and themselves, escape from the imprisonment of anger, guilt, resentment, and greed. This gives one the freedom to love and be loved.

There is also a seldom mentioned trait of shamans: cross-dressing. Both Óðinn and Þórr are depicted as cross-dressing, a reflection of oneness where male and female are not separate but symbolically united within the individual. I must confess that the story of Þórr cross-dressing in Freyja's clothes (her bridal outfit) to retrieve his hammer is entertaining while possibly containing hidden knowledge. Impersonating Freyja, Þórr dressed as a bride to fool the giant Þrymr, who wanted to marry Freyja in exchange for the return of Mjǫllnir, Þórr's hammer, which he had stolen. Could this form of cross-dressing, in a bridal gown, indicate Þórr's sacred marriage to himself—a shamanic and esoteric practice? Additionally, it's been suggested "that the eight nights of fasting and sleeplessness, which Loki uses comically to explain 'Freyja's hunger and burning eyes,' could possibly have preserved an additional remnant of shamanic practice: that is, that Þórr originally underwent this ordeal as part of a shamanic alteration of consciousness directed toward the killing of Þrymr and the reclamation of his hammer."[77]

There are other indications of Óðinn's and Þórr's connections to shamanism. The accepted text on shamanism is Mircea Eliade's *Shamanism: Archaic Techniques of Ecstasy*. "In *Shamanism*, Eliade cites Óðinn's *Hávamál* ordeal, his eight-legged horse, his shape-shifting ability (as described in Ynglinga saga chapter 7), and that of other wizards who depart their bodies and perform actions in animal shapes, and the various descents to the underworld in Norse literature as all being typical of shamanic practices…Likewise, Þórr performs several types of activities characteristic of shamans in his travels to the otherworld."[78] For example, Þórr protects the community from supernatural beings and brings back objects of power, which are of use to the community. Even Frigg and Freyja have their shamanic, feathered clothing—their falcon dresses, a motif of flying to the otherworld.

⚜

As masters of the otherworld and earth, shamans are sensitive to wood, stone, and all the elements that surround them. They look to the stars at night and to the four winds during the day. They listen to the magic roar of the streams and moaning surge of the oceans to learn the truth of the great mysteries of life. The shape of the clouds reveals the secrets of life and death. And the cry of the owl reminds them of their ancestors and the dark knowledge and wisdom of the earth.

Unlike priests, they are not gatekeepers between you and the otherworld. They are messengers, not gatekeepers. Shamans have a knowing of the mysteries of the unseen otherworld and the earth, whereas the institutionalized priest deals only with heaven, and then only secondhand. The most commonly known process of the shaman—to reach the otherworld—is done through an altered state of consciousness brought about through various means, such as extreme temperature, bathing, repetitive movement, or repetitive sound, such as drumming and chanting.

More to the point, one of the key factors of a shaman's proficiency is his or her level of sensitivity, to be open and aware of the intertwining forces of the otherworld and the earth, and the ability to access both knowledge and wisdom. At any time, a person with this level of ability may access the other-world *without outside stimulus*. The reason why this is possible? Radical non-dualism is their reality. Radical nonduality is the fundamental principle and foundation of perennial philosophy.

Since the average human mind needs to be convinced something is real when they cannot see, feel, or hear it, master shamans need to perform. In other words, they would be "tricksters," performing for their audiences with much ado, using sounds, movements, distortions of the face, and any other out-of-the-normal activity, even though it is not necessary.[79] Of course, this level of mastery does not occur overnight or without great self-sacrifice and proper training or apprenticeship with one who has walked the path before. The first step in acquiring this heightened state of shamanic and spiritual mastery begins with accepting radical nondualism. Maintaining a dualistic consciousness is a great hindrance, maybe even impossible, in reaching a level of spiritual power and mastery.

Altered State Consciousness Is One of Radical Nonduality

Over the past few decades, the surge of New Agers and neo-shamans (druids, wizards, etc.) has resulted in misinformation and ignorance to the underlying fundamental knowledge and belief of shamanism. Many of these neo-shamans sought information from Mircea Eliade's book *Shamanism*. Eliade's book is a scholarly work, and it is not based on firsthand experience. He was an observer, not an actual participant in the many cultures he observed. Subsequently, other scholars who participated in a few altered-states-of-reality ceremonies and then promoted theories and practices based on their few experiences did a great disservice to ancient paradigms of spiritual, religious, and healing thought.

Altered states of consciousness occur through various means, a few I have already mentioned. Others include hallucinogenic plants, breath control, fasting, and isolation. But these are only tools to achieve a paradigm shift in one's consciousness. This is to shift from a dualistic consciousness, where spirit and matter are separated, to one of radical nonduality. A master shaman may then access the otherworld at any time without any outside stimulus (please see my Valkyrjar tale in chapter 5).

In other words, a great disservice has been conducted by leading people down a path (based on of one's own lack of knowledge and power), where beating a drum and closing your eyes qualifies you to become a shaman or druid. What is even more maddening is sham shamans conducting *blót* with animals.

The true and narrow path to becoming a person of power—whether that person is called shaman, druid, wizard, goði or mystic—is difficult and takes years to achieve. But do not equate the tools with the state of being.

It is also important to know that there are no bad or evil spirits we need to protect ourselves from. Protection is physical and/or mental separation, which only influences and promotes the continuance of a dualistic consciousness. Energy is energy; however, there are unseen energetic forms that may attach themselves to our bodies, which may cause physical symptoms and problems that traditional medicine is not able to diagnose or heal. These vibrational energies are, in most cases, not compatible or in harmony with our vibrational bodies and minds.

Shamanic Extraction

If I were writing this book over a decade ago, this section would not be as necessary as it is today. I still would have shared cautionary thoughts about purchasing or accepting older esoteric items. But it is more important in today's world of eBay and other online auction sites. No travel to foreign lands, it's all done from the comfort of your home. But there is a problem, which you will discover or maybe already have experienced.

The majority of my sacred objects have stories connected with them and were found during my various adventures over the past thirty plus years. Not only do they carry the power of the lands they were wedded to, but they also hold my memories of time, place, and adventure. I know the circumstances surrounding them. They are not an unknown, purchased off of the Internet. But for many armchair adventurers, the memories are only of the winning bid.

Sacred items may retain the energetic memories of their previous use. This also extends to martial items, such as swords. Many factors, including how they have been used, will determine their effect on the present owner. This effect may be neutral, positive, or negative.

These effects may also stem from a spirit that has attached itself to the item. Casting out serpents is not metaphor but literal. It is a form of healing where an energetic serpent is taken off of a person and cast away. This is one of the oldest and more advanced forms of shamanic/spiritual healing. It is the hands-on healing of extracting old energies, which are usually in the form of a serpent. This energy may wrap itself around a person's limb during a time of intense trauma—most often not a physical trauma but more commonly of an emotional, mental, and/or spiritual nature. It may lie dormant for years until something triggers its activation.[80]

In the same manner, a person may trigger an item's spiritual stowaway. One story portrays this vividly. Sherry and I had flown into New York to conduct an apprentice training and were staying at an apprentice's house on Long Island. Like myself, the apprentice was a martial artist. He was also an avid buyer of items on eBay. Even though it was late at night when we finally arrived at his house and were tired having traveled all day, he still wanted to show me something as soon as we walked into his house. What he showed me was a *nodachi* or a horse sword, which was used by Japanese cavalry or foot soldiers. It is nearly a five-foot-long, two-handed sword that was basically used to take down a horse and its rider or soldiers on the ground. The apprentice handed me the sword, and within seconds, I handed it back to him.

I am not a night dreamer. Yes, I dream, and I have had some powerful dreams, but primarily I am a daytime dreamer. The next morning, I was in that twilight stage between sleeping and waking. In that gray area of existence, the dream/waking image I had was of a centipede on my back, choking me. And then I woke, gasping for air. Perspiration had formed on my forehead. Even though I was slightly shaken in both body and mind, I shrugged it off as my being overly tired from traveling and didn't think much more about it—until I took a shower.

Initially, a spirit intrusion will affect our bodies at their weakest points. I know my body, and its weakest point is my lower back. One time, when I was studying the martial arts in Japan, I unconsciously disrespected a former grandmaster of the arts by calling him by just his last name—a grave offense to any Japanese, but it was especially disrespectful to my former grandmaster. I didn't do it intentionally; it was just a slip of the tongue. When his hand touched my hand, it was stone cold and the image that popped into my mind was of writhing maggots. I hadn't even realized the disrespect until, as we were walking away, my son said, "Dad, you just called him by his last name. His whole energy changed at that moment. He was none too happy."

Within the hour, I began to feel a little dizzy and sick. I wondered, *Did he put something on me? No,* I thought, *he wouldn't have done that for a simple slip of the tongue.* Of course, he didn't know it was unintentional. Sherry and I had been taught the knowledge of extracting unwanted spirit entities as well as putting them on others, and the cold hand and wriggling maggots had all the hallmarks of this practice.

Later that night, at martial arts training with my current grandmaster, all doubt left my mind—my lower back went out for no reason at all. It was not until the next day, when the grandmaster conducted *kuji kiri* (esoteric spirit power) over me that my back got better.

Ten years after that experience, it was déjà vu. As I was taking my shower, I slightly bent over and felt the first pangs of pain. Straightening up, I quickly exited the shower, threw on some clothes, and went downstairs to find my wife.

"Sherry," I said. "Something's on my back. Would you please take it off?"

Without any hesitation, she asked, "Where can I do it?"

"Out front, next to the driveway is a tree stump. I can sit on it, and you can work on my back," I replied.

Discreetly, we excused ourselves and went outside. Once Sherry began working on me, I could feel her pulling it off. Depending on the spirit entity, this healing can become almost like an epic battle, with the healer having one foot in the otherworld and one foot in our material world. And so it seemed that Sherry was engaged in one of these struggles. There are two important parts to this form of healing. The first part is, of course, taking the entity off the person. The second part is equally important: casting it away so that it stays in the otherworld and doesn't return to the person.

I had not told Sherry about my waking experience, of a centipede choking me. She had no idea what was on me. However, I now knew that it had attached itself to me when I had held the sword. This was also why I had only handled it for a short time. Brief or not, it was still time enough for it to have taken up residence on my body. It felt my martial spirit and attached to me, not to my student.

Finally, I could feel that it was off me as Sherry cast it away. After a few minutes had passed, she said, "Wow. It didn't want to be taken off of you. And this was a first."

"What do you mean?" I replied.

"I've never come across this type of spirit. It began at the base of your spine and was all the way up to your neck. It was a giant centipede!"

There is an interesting postscript to this story. There was a special group of mounted samurai messengers called *Mukade*—centipede. These mounted warriors were supposedly known as "one worth a thousand." There weapon of choice—*nodachi*. The feudal Japanese did not think of the centipede as having positive qualities, but it was considered good luck in battle and was the battle banner of the famous general Takada Shingen. The folklore about the centipede is that they will bite you in the behind!

Initiation

Shamans are "masters of fire." In other words, they are divine smiths forging the spirit of themselves and others. "The 'mastery of fire', common both to magician, shaman and smith, was, in Christian folklore, looked upon as the work of the devil: one of the most frequently recurring popular images shows the devil spitting flames. Perhaps we have here the final mythological transformation of the archetypal image of the 'master of fire'. Odin-Wotan was the master of the *wut*, the *furor religiosus* (*Wotan, id est furor*, wrote Adam von Bremen). Now the *wut*, like other terms in the Indo-European religious vocabulary (furor, ferg, ménos), signifies the anger and extreme heat provoked by an excessive ingestion of sacred power."[81]

Shamans are also "masters of water." Both fire and water are elements of purification, rejuvenation, transmutation and initiation. After years of training the shaman demonstrates their mastery by being able to wash with fire and burn with water. In 1988 I was initiated in the sacred lagoons located on the Markawasi Plateau, Peru by the *curandero* – don Eduardo Calderon. One part of this Peruvian tradition is the transformational fire ceremony. The key ceremonial element is making the fire friendly. When I have achieved this, participants are able to wash their hands within the fire. The other aspect of shamanic power is to burn by water. This occurs when I bathe in the cold and rushing waters of a river. My body burns with an icy-fire of my awakened fiery divine spark.

The journey to achieve these abilities begins with our seeking into the unknown and through foreign lands for knowledge and power. And then comes initiation. As a form of initiation, Óðinn hung on the world tree seeking access to the knowledge and power of the otherworld:

> The myth of Odin's hanging is a myth about initiation... During the liminal phase of an initiation rite, the initiand travels – in a spiritual sense – to another world. There he acquires numinous knowledge in some form, knowledge that irreversibly alters his status when he returns to his own world. This is what happen to Odin. He hung for nine nights – the liminal phase – and returned from his ordeal with new powers....
>
> The liminal phase of an initiation rite is a symbolic death – the old persona dies and the initiand is reborn with a new persona. The point is not for the initiand to die for real, however, as in an execution... It is merely a means of gaining access to the otherworld....
>
> Hanging on the world tree is a representation of being in connection with the spiritual spheres – or maybe even of becoming that connection.[82]

When we awaken to a consciousness of radical nonduality, we become that connection:

> Like the world tree, man possesses the capability of connecting the world above with the world below. But it takes the way of the god to create the link, to tie up the connection inherit in man – a fact of which we are reminded by the name Yggdrasill and its association with the myth of Odin hanging on the world tree, and – perhaps – to the iconography of the Jelling rune stone[83].
>
> Yggdrasill's Ash may be more than the world tree, at least in *Vǫluspá*. Odin's Askr clearly indicates where man belongs – it is not with the norns. He is "man of the god", divine man, perceived as the central pillar of the Old Norse cosmos.[84]

Earth and Sky

When people feel a close connection to nature and recognize the sacredness of nature, the earth itself becomes the foundation of their temple and the sky its roof. Sacred groves, streams, rocks, and trees become our holy places. Rituals are specific to the place, honoring the divine forces felt there and the deities connected with those forces. These holy places may be marked in special ways to indicate their sacredness, with stone and/or wooden pillars, sacred woven grass ropes,[85] circles, or partial circles of stones.

For the Norse, there was no separate, organized priesthood. Their beliefs were based on a natural folk religion, not organized religion. To decipher the spiritual authority of the Norse is difficult. According to Sebastian L. Klein: "The *Goði*, or *Gyðja*, were chieftains and patrons of sacrifices in Iceland before the Icelandic conversion.... A *goði's* role in early Icelandic society was seemingly both connected to the religious sphere as well as to juridical actions undertaken at assemblies. These included choosing judges, controlling the passing of laws and initiating the assembly. The sacral duty of the *goði* was to build and maintain the *hóf* and to sponsor the rituals performed in it.... The *gyðja* is the *goði's* female counterpart. Although the *gyðja* term is not mentioned in any juridical proceedings, there are passing references in other written sources such as *Flateyjarboks'* description of the priestess of *Freyr*, who cares for its effigy and shrine."[86]

Besides the holy places in nature, there were enclosures and buildings, which functioned as religious and political spaces. As with all ancient cultures, there were ceremonies (*blót*) to feed the spirits, where animals were sacrificed. And like with other peoples, such as the Israelites, human sacrifice may have been practiced for a period of time. Within the past few years, archaeologists have discovered a pre-Christian religious site with a god temple ten kilometers north of the Norwegian city of Trondheim:

> The god temple may have been built sometime around or after the year 400 AD, thus used for hundreds of years until the people emigrated to avoid Christianity's "straitjacket." It consisted of a stone-set "sacrificial altar" and also traces of a "pole building" that probably housed idols in the form of sticks with carved faces of Þórr, Óðinn, Frey, and Freyja. Deceased relatives of high rank were also portrayed in this way and attended. Nearby, the archaeologists also uncovered a procession route.
>
> Thanks to the soil, the god temple was very well preserved. The altar, where one worshiped the gods and offered animal blood, consisted of a circular stone setting around fifteen meters in diameter and nearly a

meter high. The pole building a few meters away was rectangular, with a floor plan of 5.3 x 4.5 meters, and raised with twelve poles, each having a solid stone foundation. The building may have been high and, from the findings, was very clearly not used as a dwelling. Among other reasons, it had no fireplace. Inside the "house" were found traces of four pillars that may be evidence of a high seat where the idols stood between ceremonies. The processional road west of the temple and headed straight toward the pole building was marked with two parallel rows of large stones, the longest sequence at least twenty-five feet long.[87]

⚜

As a sign of the revival of Norse religious philosophy, Iceland is building the first heathen temple in the Nordic lands in 1000 years. According to Allsherjargoði Hilmar Örn Hilmarsson, head priest of the Icelandic Ásatrúarfélagið, the idea to build the temple "actually came up over 40 years ago, but it's something we've been planning consistently for around 12 years. We presented the proposal to the city of Reykjavik in 2003, and a few years later we were given a piece of land in the hillsides of the city. Since then, all our plans have been built around this specific location and how the sun moves around it. The temple will be finished in the autumn of 2016, and will host all our seasonal ceremonies and ritual gatherings. I'm glad to say this temple will symbolize that Ásatrú has become a perfectly acceptable part of our society, and that we are respected for our contribution to Icelandic culture."[88]

The temple will be built on a wooded hill near Reykjavik's domestic airport. Ceremonial groundbreaking for the temple was conducted on the day of a solar eclipse during the spring equinox, March 20, 2015. "The temple will provide followers of Iceland's old Norse religion with a place to hold their communal "blot" - or feasts - as well as marriages, name-giving ceremonies, funerals and rite of passage ceremonies for teenagers. Until now, ceremonies have mostly been conducted outdoors during the summer."[89]

Otherworldly Energetic Beings

As we journey from our innocence as small children to adulthood, we seemingly lose the magic before us. The wonder and beauty of the earth and all the varied creatures inhibiting our world disappear, only to be replaced by an uncompromising, unhealthy ego and the excessive need for safety, security, and materialistic consumption. Each human being is intrinsically unique, just as each tree, hummingbird, and all things of nature are inherently unique. But we miss this wonderment of creation. We see others but more in a judgmental way than in one of wonderment—of course, these are the seeds of bigotry.

Yes, we are all intrinsically different, but on the other hand, we are all the same. We all have the starlight of the divine within us. In this respect, the otherworld is no different than our own. The unknown numbers of otherworldly beings are all intrinsically unique but also the same. A Norse goddess such as Freyja is real and different in an intrinsic, energetic way from the being that the Norse identify as Freyr, her brother. We have to be careful to distinguish between mythological beings that are forces or powers of nature and ones that are truly energetic beings of the otherworld. Many times, we may not be able to distinguish between the two. Each of these, whether forces of nature or actual energetic beings, has lessons for us in evolving our soul's vibrational energy. Their identity is not as important as what they have to teach us. As an example, Tyr is the warrior god of justice. If we have focused our attention on him (see below, in Gender Neutral) such as through imagery and meditation and understand his rune and the myths connected with Tyr, we would be in a position to embrace his energy in a noble cause against an injustice. We could also just as easily call on him to assist us with issues of discipline and courage.

Gender Neutral

In our quest for primordial knowledge, it is important to keep in mind the nongendered identity of the otherworld within its intrinsic gendered identity. This is one of the reasons why I use the terms *absolute* (spirit) and *relative* (matter) at various times. Thus, no gender is assigned.

However, from our human viewpoint, it is appropriate for our understanding to assign gender to the otherworld as long as we keep in mind that they are gender neutral. For instance, in one of the many faces Óðinn wears, I would identify him as male in helping to understand his intrinsic identity. This is the same with Freyja and Frigg. Identifying these energetic beings as female is appropriate for our understanding and seeking primordial knowledge and wisdom. They can symbolically be Mother Nature.

One of the essential means to awakening is to see all other people first and foremost as human beings with the divine starlight within them before identifying them in their intrinsic dualistic identity as male or female or by their race (in reality there is only one race—the human race). But first, we need to see them as divine human beings. This will begin shifting our consciousness from a dualistic mind-set to one of radical nondualism.

Primordial knowledge was rooted in a culture that was gender neutral. It was not a patriarchal or matriarchal society. With the new Age of Aquarius, we are not leaving a god-ruled earth to become goddess ruled. Aquarius is the age of equality, when gods and goddesses rule equally in religious and spiritual thought, along with the acknowledgment that the divine resides within all things.

Dísir

The *dísir* are generally thought of as different manifestations of female deities. They seem to be a combination of deity and spirit. These supernatural beings were, in some ways, similar to the common shamanic concept of a guardian spirit. The *dísir* were otherworldly guardian women such as the *fylgjur* (follower fetch), who could be a woman or an animal. Additionally, there were guardian Valkyries and the *hamingja*, who were connected with the Norse concept of luck. The *hamingja* personify the idea of good fortune connected with an individual. Finally, there are the three sisters or the *Norns*, who may be viewed as the *hamingja* of the world, as they care for its destiny. As I noted above, it is appropriate for us to identify *dísir* as female considering their attributes as part of Mother Nature.

The Icelandic *Huldufólk* (Hidden Ones)

After my firsthand physical experience with otherworldly energetic beings in 1997, I concluded that there would also be earthly energetic beings, commonly referred to as faeries and elves. This conclusion came from my experience, and many Otherworldly experiences from an intuitive sense, scholarly knowledge, and oral teachings from elders around the world. My family and I experienced items missing and later showing up after journeying to Cornwall, England, in the nineties, a trait of the Cornish faeries known as *piskies*. As with life, it might not have been the piskies playing tricks on us but our own human forgetfulness. But then...

I had journeyed to Iceland with my son and one of our students. For the first part of our journey, we were exploring the most magical region of Iceland, Snaefellsnes, a peninsula, and its volcano, Snaefellsjokull. Jules Verne used this volcano as the setting for his novel A Journey to the Centre of the Earth. This is a mystical and strange land, where the hidden ones, elves and dwarves, hide in dark crevices and caves while strange rock formations are ogres and trolls. This is the land of fire and ice. It is nature in all its glory, creative and destructive though it may be. The wind, the sea, and the hundreds of waterfalls vibrate a song of primal pureness seldom found on our beautiful but wounded earth.

It is important to follow a few spiritual protocols. These are not dogma and doctrine based but more rooted in common sense and respect for the spirit world. Asking the otherworld's permission when conducting our spirit work is one protocol that we follow faithfully and teach to our students. When we travel to a new place or return to one, it is best to do prayers, an offering, which could be as simple as a piece of our hair, and ask permission to be there and do our work. I also ask for safety for myself and others while we are on our journey. Sometimes this rite is short and simple, and at other times more extensive and intense. There is no format to follow, just your heart. As soon as I set foot in this magical land, I felt a strong connection and kinship. For this reason, early the next morning, facing the cloud-covered volcano with the icy winds crashing into me, I did an extensive and complete rite of permission. At least I thought I did.

It is virgin land in the sense that the New Agers have not discovered it and few tourists spend any time there. It is not only unspoiled land, but it is home to many legends and myths and one of the most famous Icelandic Viking shamans, Bárður. This legendary shaman was born in northern Norway and his grandmother was a Sami who passed on her shamanic and magical knowledge to him. One of the sacred sites on the edge of the volcano is known as the Singing Cave. This is Bárður's cave, where he would spend time conducting his shamanic practice.

Since it was October, a time of the year for few tourists, we were just about guaranteed to be the only ones visiting the various sacred sites on the peninsula. Late in the afternoon, on the second day, we spent time in the Singing Cave. As its name indicates, one of the most obvious and important practices to conduct here would be *galdr*—Norse magical chant/song. Once again, I needed to make myself known to the spirit world and ask permission to enter the cave and do our work. Once inside, I conducted a blessing, an honoring and opening ceremony. Then we proceeded with other practices including an old magical chant. The sound of our voices vibrated off the cave walls, and once more, Bárður's cave was singing.

We spent another day and half on the peninsula before we returned to Reykjavik, the capital of Iceland. While in Reykjavik, we stayed at the Grand Hotel, which would be our residence for the final days of our journey. The Grand Hotel is beautiful. However, I did not choose it for its beauty but for the Grand Hotel's honoring of Norse mythology. When you enter the hotel, you are greeted with a phenomenal piece of glass artwork portraying the creation of the world based on the "Völuspá." Their front desk is decorated with small poems from the *Poetic Edda*'s "Hávamál," which provides advice for living, proper conduct, and wisdom. Staying there captured the feeling and essence of the Norse who had settled there after leaving Norway.

My room was on the twelfth floor overlooking the ocean and the fog-covered Snaefellsnes. Even though the hotel's focus was on mythology, it was your typical, ordinary hotel...or so I thought. The next day, we were leaving early to explore Thingvellir National Park, where Iceland's parliament, Althing, was founded. Heeding the advice "early to bed, early to rise," I turned in around ten o'clock. I had only been asleep a few minutes before the phone began ringing. After I answered it, a voice said, "I'm calling to make sure the four Russians we sent over arrived safely since we're overbooked here." I told them they'd reached a private room and not the front desk and promptly hung up to keep myself from totally waking up. A few more minutes passed, and the phone rang again.

This time, the voice spoke Icelandic until I explained I didn't understand, and they finally said in English, "This is not the front desk?" Hanging up once again and crawling back to bed, I thought, *What is going on?*

The phone ran constantly until I wised up and unplugged it at two in the morning. The next morning after breakfast, I plugged the phone back in and once again the calls began, all wanting information from the front desk. Realizing it was not a fluke, I informed the front desk about the strange occurrence. They apologized and said that they would look into it, stating that it had never happened before and was seemingly impossible.

After a full day of exploring Thingvellir, I checked in at the front desk before going back to my room. The problem had been fixed, but there was no explanation for how it had happened. There was no logical reason to explain it. Later that night, as I was pondering this mystery, it finally came to me—the hidden ones. I had forgotten to include them in my prayers. And they will let you know if they have been offended or slighted in some manner. I immediately did prayers and an offering to them. The result: the rest of our journey was uneventful.

Is this the end of my story? Not at all. It seems that one or more decided to hop a ride on our flight home and now reside with us on another peninsula—this one in Washington state, overlooking the only fjord in the western continental United States!

Loki—A Hidden One?

Nine months later (interesting number, huh?) we had a very young feral cat show up at our back door. During one of its morning feedings, he bit me very deeply. It was my fault, as I frightened him when I turned over his feeding dish. Common sense dictated a visit to the physician. Of course, the thought within the physician's mind was rabies. He emphasized that I needed to trap the cat to discover if it had rabies. I replied I didn't want to, as he was living outside our home. "Well," he said, "the cat may get hit by a truck and you will not know until it is too late if it was rabid, as rabies untreated will kill you."

My wife and I decided not to trap it to discover if it was rabid but to trap it due to a wicked-looking injury near his tail and his dreadful appearance. Let's just say that he was very wild. In fact, after trapped and taken to a vet, the rescue cat woman felt that he might be better off as a mouser at one of the farms but asked if we would like him back.

We decided to take him back to our home and let him loose, where we were hoping he would stick around, which he did. Of course, getting regular meals, why wouldn't he? Add to this our home's location—overlooking a fjord with eagles, coyotes, mountain lions, and bears in the vicinity of our home. Staying close could mean life over death.

A month passed with our feral cat still outside our home. And then came the night of July 4—and fireworks. Where my wife was sitting, she could see our barbecue, which was outside on our back deck. Sitting on it, looking in at my wife, was the shivering, scared little cat who, by now, had put on weight.

We opened the sliding glass door, and with no hesitation, he ran in and became a part of our family, which also included three other cats, all three strays/feral including one Maine Coon cat, a Viking cat.

The next day, Sherry named him Loki. It was as if someone had whispered his name into her ear. This was a name we would not have chosen for him. At that time, we did not even know his breed. Amazingly, Loki adapted to our home rapidly. In fact, after a few weeks, you wouldn't have even believed that he had ever been a feral cat.

Within a short period, we knew Loki was different from your average cat, feral or otherwise. His behaviors and eyes were strange to say the least. Loki had a baby face but was large for one so young. In my research for this book and on a journey to Norway and Iceland, I stumbled across Loki's breed—*Norsk Skogkatt*, Norwegian Forest Cat. It seemed that another Viking cat had found us, even though there were no known Norwegian Forest Cats in Western Washington state.

The mystery and essence—yes essence—of the enigmatic Loki does not stop here. It is his eyes—they are otherworldly and of this world. Eyes are the portals to the soul, and researching the Norwegian Forest Cat, I discovered something that shed some light on our mysterious Loki. Deeply rooted in Norse mythology, "the Norwegian Forest Cat (*Norsk Skogkatt*) is the gift of the Norse gods to the cat kingdom. Celebrated in Norse mythology and nineteenth century Nordic fables, this cat has an air of enchantment. It has awed Þórr and pulled Freya's chariot. Asbjomsen and Moe embellished their Norwegian fairy tales with descriptions of these 'huge and furry Troll cats.'"[90]

Mystery solved—Loki was a faerie cat! And it all made sense. At certain times, he was not of this world, his eyes actually changing into Otherworldly orbs—a trait noticed not only by us but by others. Could it be possible that our dear Loki has the spirit of the hidden ones within him? Maybe not...but then...maybe so. And then there is this: in Denmark, these cats are called *huldrekat*—hidden folk!

Triple Goddess—the Wisdom of the Nornir

> *"The two most important days in your life are the*
> *day you are born and the day you find out why."*
> —MARK TWAIN

To achieve power and wisdom, we must discover our true path in life and follow it. There is joy in our true identities as we fulfill our destiny in life. With a "mind that listens and a heart that sees," everything in life is sacred, and every action is hallowed. There is no stagnation in our life, only movement. This movement is always toward destiny and away from the mediocrity of a life that has been lived in blindness and deafness.

Fate and destiny are complex concepts that few focus on in our society, more interested in materialistic gain, power, control, and greed. Just as everyone has a divine spark, everyone's shared destiny is physical death. When we accept life, we accept death, but out of death there is life. Individually, we do have an intrinsic destiny, or mission if you wish. This is a mystery few seek to know. Philosophically, our intrinsic destiny is intertwined with our fate based on achieving a level of soul evolution. But our fates are not individual threads. They are intertwined with all other things, not just the ones in our immediate environment.

The Norse-Germanic concepts of fate and destiny are termed in Old Norse urðr (Old English wyrd) and ørlög meaning ancient or primal law. Ørlög is the unchangeable aspects of our birth, such as our parents and our DNA (earthly and heavenly—our past-lives). Whereas urðr is the concept of fate that may be changed. We take what is given to us and then we forge (or maybe not) our spirit through our choices in life and our thoughts, words and deeds.

In regard to fate and destiny, I do not buy into some people's concept of karma, where we are being punished for actions in past lifetimes, nor the Christian concept of grace, where we are at the mercy of gifts from God. On the other hand, from a philosophical standpoint, I believe the Norse-Germanic concept of fate and destiny to be one of the best paradigms to consider. It is based on a triple goddess paradigm, the *Nornir*, and intertwined with two of their basic cosmologic symbols—the world tree and the well - *Urðarbrunnr* or "the spring of Urðr, commonly translated as the past. However, the real meaning of the name is Origin, primal cause, the connotation being that of antecedent causes from which flow all subsequent effects."[91]

The yew tree, Yggdrasill, is metaphorically the center of the seen and unseen universe. It holds the nine worlds of Norse mythology. Within Yggdrasill's branches and roots dwell all things of creation, all sentient beings and things of the seen and unseen world.

Yggdrasill is watered by the well of Urðr. This is extremely important, as water is a central to life. The water nourishes the tree and all the worlds, and its fir branches shed this water by dripping dewdrops back into the well, re-plenishing it. This is the archetypal water cycle discovered in the esoteric lore of many culture.

Water is life. One reason life exists on earth is due to the natural water cycle of our planet: water evaporates from the surface of the ocean; moist air raises; it cools, and water vapor condenses to form clouds; the moisture is transported around the globe until it returns to the surface as precipitation. The earth's water cycle is even alluded to in the Hebrew Tanakh, in Ecclesiastes 1:7: "All streams flow into the sea, yet the sea is never full; to the place [from] which they flow, the streams flow back again."

Furthermore, in our journey to awaken, the imagery of the world tree's wa-ter cycle points us to certain esoteric truths. One is time—a circular passage of time as well an interpenetration of time where timelessness and linear time are one. This is not a linear sequence of past, present, and future. It is the influence of the past on the present and the present influencing the past (forgiveness/transforming patterns), which then have an effect on our present and destiny. By combining this concept of the circular passage of time with the concepts of linear time and timelessness, we have a better grasp of the truth of existence and consciousness.

We reflect the cycles of nature—birth, death, rebirth, and becoming. We are becoming. The influence of the present on the past basically means a new present. It is easy to shove the past into the deepest, darkest recesses of our consciousness, which many do. To the Norse, this act is pure stupidity. Since the present is symbolized by Yggdrasill, while the past is the well of Urðr, we can influence the waters that feed our personal tree of life. Letting the waters stagnate does not provide for the well-being of our metaphoric brothers and sisters, our tree, or our awakening.

The attendants at the well are the three sisters: the *Nornir*— Urðr (ori-gin/fate/"that which is"), Verdandi (being/becoming), and Skuld (necessity/debt). At birth, the Nornir carve our lives' journeys and destinies into the tree. All things are subject to these carvings. But different than most paradigms, these carvings are not absolute and may be altered. In other words, all beings have a degree of power over their destiny as well as other's destinies. A key to awakening is being more active and powerful in shaping our destiny, with the understanding that we are still subject to necessity. Necessity links us with the concept of weaving. Everything is interconnected in a web of creation; everything interpenetrates; everything is one.

Skuld, or necessity, may be viewed as a seed that needs to germinate. For the human race, this would be the seed of light or spark of awakening. This is necessity from our soul's perspective. In Old Norse, *skuld* means "debt, bondage in payment of debt." It is derived from *skulu*, which means "shall" or "must." In other words, this is what we shall or will do—germinate the seed. Our seed of light, our heavenly lineage, is not the only seed of Skuld. The other is our earthly lineage, or our seed of our ancestors. Life is struggle and philosophically, life is bondage to an extent. The only hell we may experience is right here on earth while we are alive. But, by awakening, we loosen the ties that bind us.

Verdandi, or being, symbolizes the present from the Norse verb *verda*—to become. This is where we become aware of the seeds and awaken them. Urðr, or fate, is our spiritual destiny or soul path and symbolizes the past not only our seeds of Necessity but seeds we've produced through our actions that are "debts" that need to be repaid.

Another manner in which to view these concepts is by portraying Urðr as personifying "all that has gone before and is the cause of both present and future. Verdandi is the present, but it is not a static condition; on the contrary, it means becoming—the dynamic, ever-changing, mathematical point between past and future, a point of vital importance for it is the eternal moment of choice for humans, when conscious willing decision is made, directed by desire, either for progress or retrogression on the evolutionary path. It is noteworthy that these two Norns create the third, Skuld, meaning *debt*: something owed, out of balance, to be brought into equilibrium in the future—the inevitable result of all the past and of the present."[92]

Harmony, movement, and action—right action—is essential to these concepts. This is not Descartes's philosophy based solely on humans: "I think; therefore I exist." But a universal philosophy of "I act; therefore I exist" or even more profound: "I consciously act; therefore I exist." The greatest action we do is breathing—I exist. I breathe. This philosophy takes into account all things of creation, not just humans, as Desecrate would have you believe.

To assist in making this knowledge a part of your life, I have a question for you to ponder: What debts do you need to repay?

Deeds Trump Words

One of the most important legacies of the Norse-Germanic cultures was the emphasis on deeds, which is contrary to the present day and the Christian usurpers of the past and present, when words are spoken with no action taken. Talk is cheap. Deeds may be an expression of power for the benefit of others, such as kin and community. Conversely, this power may be based on greed, materialistic gain, or control over others—witness the deeds of Charlemagne, who massacred some 4,500 Saxon prisoners, destroyed heathen places of worship, and decreed the death penalty for all those who refused to be baptized or those who continued to practice the pagan faith.

Deeds based on qualities and values of spirit, self, community, and the welfare of others and the earth is the focus of this book. These are the deeds and actions to awaken our own inner power to overcome our life's struggles and to help others and return a green philosophy to the consciousness of humanity.

Movement/Nonmovement vs. Good and Bad

First off, the Norse-Germanic people had no concept similar to Christianity's original sin. Additionally, their concept of good and bad was philosophically different from today's religiously influenced dualistic mind-set of good and bad. Instead, they considered movement or action essential to the well-being of all things. This concept was rooted and related to the movement of the sacred waters boiling up from *Urðarbrunnr* throughout the total essence of Yggdrasill. Movement or action was reflected in all aspects of life within Midgard from the cycles of nature to the tides of the sea and cycles of the moon.

Movement was the key to life throughout the width and breath of Yggdrasill and would symbolize our concept of good or positive. Of course then, non-movement or inaction would be looked upon as bad or, if you will, sinful or evil. According to Eric Wódening referring to Paul Bauschatz's book *The Well and the Tree* states, "the Germanic people viewed stasis or inaction as negative and movement or action as positive. Bauschatz insisted this concept was typified by the interaction between the Well and the Tree."[93]

We may see the impact of a shift in mind-set from an individual's concept of good and bad to movement and nonmovement in countless ways. As an example, good and bad is rooted more in personal judgment, based possibly on prejudice, dogma, or doctrine. On the other hand, action or inaction is pretty straight forward, as there is no room for judgment; there is either movement or no movement. As an example, in a community setting, "inaction on the parts of individuals could affect the survival of a community. The man who out of sloth failed to do his share of the harvest or the man who out of cowardice did not join in battle beside his tribesman could cost lives through his inaction. These are crimes in which the individual has not so much committed a wrong as he has failed to do what is right. In other words, he has failed to act. An inaction is usually not beneficial to the community and does nothing to maintain the community."[94]

A present day example would be a dysfunctional marriage where both partners ignore the dysfunction and keep the relationship static with no action toward resolving the roots of the dysfunction. This inaction would affect any children within the family and the extended family. Movement would involve a change of behaviors of both, possibly counseling, and, if need be, separation or divorce.

Reflect on your life and see if there is any area where there is inaction. Then, in the spirit of "deeds not words," institute movement and change/transformation.

⚜

One last point: this concept of movement was to be found within Mesoamerican thought and belief. It was known as the "heart that sees," which was called Ollin in their tradition. This symbolized the "motion principle" in Mesoamerican thought, but in addition, it had the meaning of having a purified heart or a "heart that sees" truth. It is a compassionate heart that sees everything in life as sacred and every action we take as hallowed. There is no stagnation in our lives, only movement. This movement is always toward destiny or becoming and away from the mediocrity of a life that has been lived in self-blindness and stagnation.

Know Thyself

Knowing ourselves means recognizing, first and foremost, that we are divine human beings. We are not sinful human beings but divine humans. Our divine spark interpenetrates our humanness—body, mind, and spirit. The absolute interpenetrates the relative.

This is the first step in knowing ourselves and realizing that each of us is a microcosm of the macrocosm. In other words, know thyself and thou shall know the universe and the gods and goddesses. To awaken, we must know ourselves and all other things—not only with our minds but also with our hearts and our experiences in life. This is self-knowledge rooted in experiencing the mysteries of life or *participation mystique*. When we know ourselves, we will know the Kingdom of Óðinn as Allfather within us and the Kingdom of Óðinn as Allfather outside us.[95]

As divine human beings, we are responsible for our behaviors and actions. There is no distant and far away deity to blame or to seek some form of dogmatic salvation from. Each of us has direct access to the mysteries of heaven (Otherworld) and earth (our world). There is no need of priestly intermediaries between us and the mysteries of body, mind, spirit, and soul.

The constant counter argument to these philosophical statements is often: If we have divineness within us, why do humans commit the atrocities (slaughter of adults, children, and even babies; rape; torture; needless destruction of the earth and its creatures; etc.) that have happened for millennia? The answer is quite simple: yes, we are born with a divine spark, but our divineness is unawakened. Knowing this and the realization that we are still humans with bodies, minds, emotions, and spirits, and we will always have the choice of right action, wrong action, a combination of both, or inaction. In other words, even after we awaken our divineness, we will still make human mistakes and possibly act in ways that are not true and right. Knowing ourselves means that we will love and we will fear; we will struggle and suffer, and we will have joy and happiness; we will live, and we will die. This is a knowing of ourselves and then striving to become more divine with as little human wrongdoing as possible. The following chapters will assist you in discovering the totality of you.

Participation Mystique

Since the dawn of time, the purpose of life, religion, and spirituality was not to be centered in faith, belief, or a sacred book but in participation mystique. This is a knowing of the things of life and their inherent mysteries through the experience of the mundane as well as the spiritual. The emphasis is on a direct experience with the totality of body and mind and not just the intellect. It is an immersion in the mysteries of nature and the seeking of knowledge through mystical participation. This "doing" may be as simple as sitting alone under a tree and listening to the sounds of nature and our own heart or as complex as bathing in a stream at dawn. This participation mystique will result in a transformation of consciousness.

Myth and Symbolism—Keys to the Mysteries of the Otherworld

According to Joseph Campbell, there are basically four functions to myth. First is a mystical function. Second is a cosmological function, which is followed by a sociological one. The fourth function is most important in our return to a green philosophy. This fourth function is a pedagogical function: "how to live a human lifetime under any circumstances. Myths can teach you that."[96] This function is the meat of the following three chapters.

Mythic gods and goddesses are "personifications of a motivating power or a value system that functions in human life and in the universe—the powers of your own body and of nature. The myths are metaphorical of spiritual potentiality in the human being, and the same powers that animate our life animate the life of the world."[97] Keep in mind that Otherworldly beings are energetic and real.

⚜

Symbols are part and partial of our everyday lives and are an entrenched culture within capitalistic and religious institutions. Bluetooth's logo or symbol is a combination of two runes of the Younger Fuþąrk—hagall and bjarkan. Consider USB's icon. It resembles Poseidon's trident, with the three primary shapes of a triangle, square, and circle instead of three spear points. Religiously, Catholic bishop's hats symbolize a fish head, and the yarmulke (beanie) on Jews symbolizes a respect for God.

Hinduism and Esoteric Buddhism make extensive use of symbolism. One such example is the Buddhist Bosatsu Kannon (Chinese Kuan Yin). Kannon is known as the compassionate one. He/she hears the cries of all beings for release from their suffering.

There are also many different manifestations of Kannon, such as the Thousand (perfection or completeness) Handed or Senju Kannon. The thousand hands (reaching out far and wide to alleviate suffering) have an eye in each palm, which represents the wisdom to know what each being needs in order to aid and guide them. A hidden teaching reveals that if one eye attaches, all other eyes are useless.

If we utilize this method of symbolism with the Norse gods and goddesses, could the slouchy hat that Ódhinn wears possibly symbolize him as the keeper of mysteries/secret knowledge? Or could it possibly be the teaching not to judge a stranger on how they look?

⚜

Otherworldly beings, such as the gods and goddesses, are usually depicted in various manners, all of which are symbolic. They are associated with various animals, such as the forest cats that pull Freyja's wagon, and items like Heimdall's "ringing" horn, Gjallarhorn, which could be heard throughout heaven, earth, and the lower world.

This symbolism is a masking of the knowledge, wisdom, and power of the gods and goddesses and their relationships to us in our journey of awakening and returning to a green philosophy. Even the sagas tell us tales about mythic heroes, possibly based on real people. These also contain knowledge and truth behind their masks of symbolism.

In conclusion, the following final three chapters delve into the mysteries and the knowledge of Freyja, Þórr, and Óðinn. Within the trinity of body, mind, and spirit, I assign and symbolize body to Freyja, mind to Þórr, and spirit to Óðinn.

Freyja
Power of Nature

CHAPTER 5

Freyja

When I classify Freyja as symbolic of the body within the trinity of body, mind, and spirit, *body* refers not only to our physical bodies but also to the great body of the earth and the cosmos—Mother Nature. Additionally, we may think of Freyja's power as the power of the heart—the heart of the earth. Without our hearts—and of course ours mind and spirits—our bodies are nothing more than inert matter.

One of the mysteries of Norse lore is the differing identities of Freyja and Frigg. Their similarities cause confusion in deciphering qualities and purposes. It is my belief that they are one and the same but with an important difference. "Frigg is the highest goddess of the Æsir, while Freyja is the highest goddess of the Vanir. Many arguments have been made both for and against the idea that Frigg and Freyja are really the same goddess...There are clearly many similarities between the two: both had flying cloaks of falcon feathers and engaged in shape-shifting, Frigg was married to Odin while Freyja was married to Óðr, both had special necklaces, both had a personification of the Earth as a parent, both were called upon for assistance in childbirth, etc."[98] Furthermore, according to Rudolf Simek, "The most obvious explanation is to identify Óðr with Odin; the similarity of the names (which show a parallel with Ullr/Ullinn), the long absence, and his marriage with Freyja (whom *Grimnismal* 14 identifies with Frigg, Odin's wife) support this suggestion."[99]

Where does all of this lead us? My conclusion is that they were one and the same, originating from a common goddess—Mother Nature of creation—and Frigg is Mother Nature of the cosmos (the macrocosm) while Freyja is Mother Nature of the Earth (the microcosm).

Lady

Lady is Freyja's title. Her brother, Freyr, held the title of *Lord*. As sister and brother, they symbolize the dualistic aspects of nature. If we delve into the descriptive aspects of Freyja, we open a portal to knowledge concerning nature and life. One important point: she represents the blended aspects of life.

Freyja seems to be the most prominent goddess of the Æsir and Vanir. She is the goddess of beauty—think of the pristine beauty of nature and nature in its rawest expression. Of course, Freyja is also the goddess of love. But what is love? Is it lust or a caring and respectful attitude toward others, including nature? In Freyja's case, she is both the goddess of mundane (sensual/sexual) love and the love of sacred sexuality with the addition that she also represents the love of nature and its bounty.

In other words, Freyja symbolizes the fertility of life and nature—a giving goddess bestowing bounty to the fields, land, and animals. She is the goddess of love but also a warrior goddess. "According to both 'Grímnismál' and 'Gylfaginning,' Freyja owns the hall Sessrumnir (Many-seats) which stands on Folkvangr (the People's plain). There, she welcomes half of the war fallen. Odin receives the other half into Valhalla. Thus, Freyja was associated not only with procreation and childbirth, but also with death and the afterlife, completing the full circle of the life cycle."[100]

Freyja's/Frigg's day is Friday, symbolizing her identity as the goddess of love—Venus. The Norse name for the planet Venus is *Friggjarstjarna* (Frigg's star). Venus has two faces, one as the morning star and one as the evening star, symbolic of Freyja as warrior goddess (morning-star phase) and love goddess (evening-star phase). Another option could be Frigg as evening star and Freyja as the period during which Venus is the morning star.

As the daughter of Njörðr, she is associated with the sea and known as Mardöll (sea shimmer). Njörðr is a god of the Vanir and connected to the sea, seafaring, wind, fishing, wealth, and crop fertility. Njörðr, Freyja, and Freyr are the most prominent deities of the Vanir, symbolizing all aspects of wealth and fertility.

Quite independent and unpredictable as the sea, Freyja deals with the dead and the afterlife as queen of the Valkyries. Freyja's other shamanic connection is her falcon skin that she uses to fly and her birthing the magical art of seiðr. She taught this magic of transformation and divination to the Æsir.

Reflecting nature's power, Freyja was connected with butterflies, nature's embodiment of transformation and transcendence. Butterflies symbolize a journey of freedom—freedom from the restrictions in life to embracing and expressing the beauty of our heart and soul. And we must not forget about her large cats that pull her wagon through the sky. In the present day, these fierce and loyal cats are known as *Norsk Skogkatts* in their native Norway. These are faerie felines that very well may bring us messages from Freyja. Any stray that shows up on your doorstep, *Norsk Skogkatts* or not, may possibly be a gift from Freyja.

Last but not least is her beautiful necklace, Brísingamen, symbolizing her connection to wealth, gold, and amber. Her husband was Óðr, the aspect of sunshine, who often went away on long journeys (Could this symbolize the lack of sunlight during the winter in the Northern climes?). This resulted in Freyja crying red-golden tears for him. As her tears fell on the earth, they became gold, and the ones that fell in the sea became amber. Óðr may also mean "song" and "inspiration." It makes sense that Óðr represents sunshine that impregnates the earth, increasing the fertility of all things. Sunshine has the innate power to inspire us and sing out our happiness. Freyja's connection to wealth leads us to the first rune of the Elder Futhark.

First Rune—Fehu

Fehu is Freyja/Frigg's rune (mystery, secret knowledge, a song, a spell, a magical symbol). It is also the rune of Njörðr and Freyr. Keep in mind the Norse-Germanic cosmology of the blending of fire and ice. Fehu is the rune of primal fire that lies hidden within most people—this is the divine spark that needs to be awakened. It is the rune of fertility, abundance, and productivity through inspiration and creativity. In other words, Fehu is the rune of wealth. It is the first rune, and on some levels, it is similar to the first chakra. *Chakras* are wheels of energy. The original name meant "discus," as in the lethal throwing weapon, with the meaning of destroying the passions that hinder a person's journey toward enlightenment. Passions in this case refers to anything that disrupts the tranquility of the mind.

It is believed that chakras are depositories of memory. Our emotional woundings and the past issues connected with those woundings may be locked away within the various chakras. These blockages will definitely affect and inhibit the energy flow throughout our body. Over time, this disharmony will affect the body's various health systems and will ultimately result in a state of unhappiness and disease. The first chakra could be viewed as the wealth chakra. It is located at the base of the spine and deals with issues of safety, security, basic needs, basic human survival, profane sex, and inappropriate sexual activity (unawakened beast) and one's sense of roots, family, and connection to the earth (an unawakened first chakra views earth/nature as hostile). This is the chakra of dualism as well as the endocrine system, reproductive glands, and adrenals. The color symbolism is red.

Of course, people equate wealth with safety, security, basic needs, and human survival. The need for excessive amounts of wealth/money and the sacrifice of spirit and family that comes with it has never made sense to my consciousness. It seems as if a person has one million, then they believe they need two million and then five, and that turns into ten million; the need for more wealth seemingly never ends. Why would a person who has even a million or millions keep being a slave to money with endless hours of work? I know people believe in original sin. This gives the indication that they are flawed; they're bad. Maybe they believe wealth will reverse this flaw. I wonder how things would change if people believed in original divinity not original sin? The realization of our divine selves, not sinful selves, would be the understanding that true wealth is internal not external.

I know there is a sense of power that comes with external wealth. But external power, without an equal amount of internal power of spirit and heart, corrupts. And then there is the endless work ethic—work first, family second. Is this all there is to life? How about a family-life ethos, where the majority of one's time is spent with family instead of working to achieve more money and things? At least the European cultures recognize the need for holiday (holy-day) and receive at least four to six weeks of time off.

The key to the reason behind people's need for excessive money is found within the knowledge of Fehu. Fehu symbolizes kinsmen's strife, flood's fire, and serpent's path. It is the rune of primal fire, creative fire/inspiration, wealth/prosperity, outer and inner wealth, and soul gains from a life well lived.

Fehu symbolizes the mythological dragon and its horde of gold and jewels. It connotes the mystery of gold where the focus is on money (outer wealth) or awakening (inner wealth). This inner or outer gold increases in power through circulation. However, true wealth is to be found in a life full of right action of generosity, love, and compassion flowing from our hearts—our inner gold—not from the excesses of wealth or material accumulation.

Fehu cautions that earthly goods are a joy to humans, but also cause strife among kin and others. The path of the serpent is symbolized by the lind-worm (Norse dragon/wingless serpent) in its ability to make the wealth of the owner grow. Sounds good, but on the other hand, there is a hidden trap. As the wealth grows, the serpent grows equally. This results in the need for more wealth (greed). The result is an endless cycle for more wealth and power. In Christian terms, you have sold your soul to the devil.

A question to ponder: Which are you primarily growing—spirit or money? Why?

Body and Soul

To the Norse-Germanic mind, body and soul were not dualistic concepts but were united as one. If you hugged a tree, you were not only holding its body, but you were also embracing its essence—its soul:

> All peoples recognize a body and a soul, or rather a material and a spiritual side to everything that exists. The bird has a body which is lifted in the air, and it has a soul which enables it to fly, as well as to strike with its beak. So also the stone is a body, but in this body there is a soul that wills and enables the stone to do harm, to bite and strike and crush; a soul which gives it its hardness, its rolling movement, its power of prophesying the weather or showing the way...
>
> To find the soul, wherever we grasp, be it stone or beast or tree, we lay hold of it. It comes toward us conscious of itself, as a thing that knows and wills, acts and suffers—in other words, as a personality.[101]

Everything has a soul/spirit within its outward form. In other words, spirit and matter interpenetrate where everything has a divine spark and consciousness within it. Everything is alive and conscious. This knowledge motivated the Norse to become partners with their surroundings—to win friendship with the souls/powers of the animals, trees, and stones, and to establish an inner relationship with them. Their life was not only connected with the powers of the earth but to the unseen powers of the cosmos and earth—the totality of Yggdrasill.

This weaving of life together created a web of *frith* ("peace" – "calm"). According to Vilhelm Grönbech, "The key-note of ancient culture is not conflict, neither is it mastery, but conciliation and friendship. Man strives to make peace with the animals, the trees, and the powers that be, or deeper still, he wants to draw them into himself and make them kin of his kin, till he is unable to draw a fast line between his own life and that of the surrounding nature."[102]

This statement may seem strange concerning conflict, as the prevailing, but changing, view of the Vikings is as bloodthirsty pirates. We know this is not totally true, as the conflict was forced on them by the brutal incursion of Christianity. Their basic philosophy was *frith*—freedom and friendship as the foundation of their soul. The Norse were primarily farmers, adventurers, and people of the sea. Their level of warrior skill came from common sense intelligence and a spirit and philosophy of fate/life/death/reincarnation. It was not by a need for conflict based on converting other cultures and societies to their religion, or by an enforced, structured military training, where there was an absence of a philosophical belief in fate and reincarnation—conflict lacking such a philosophy of fate and reincarnation will only result in a person having an inhibiting fear of death resulting in a fearful spirit. The Norse accepted death. The result was fierce warriors who depended on their brothers and sisters in the shield wall. The only other warrior culture with this mind-set was the ancient Spartans.

Megin

Humans may be viewed as having four souls: *fjör* – self/immortal soul, *megin*, *hugr*, *mód* – mind. "Each of these four nevertheless contains at every moment its fellow souls, and is responsible for them in every point. Indeed, in the deepest foundation of the matter, they are not separated at all."[103]

One of these manifestations of the soul is *megin*. This equates to the intrinsic idea of power. The soul of rivers, waterfalls, seas—its megin—is the power of transformation, cleansing, and purification. The earth has megin, and so does the weather, the sun, the moon, and so forth. It is strength, power, and ability—inner power of all things. Divine power—power of the gods and goddesses—was referred to as *regin*. "As power or luck, the gods are in Old Norse called *ráð* and *regin*; *ráð* means *rede*: wisdom and will, the power of determining and powerful determinations; *regin* simply expresses luck and power."[104]

Hugr

Spirit and *soul* often cause confusion as to their meaning and purpose. Our soul is immortal, while our spirit is earthbound, connected with our present incarnation. The spirit can be thought of as the essential nature of a person, for example, that person has a kindly spirit. To an extent, spirit is a reflection of our souls, and of course, of our minds, which leads us to *hugr*. *Hugr* may be viewed "as desire and inclination, as courage and thought. It inspires a man's behavior; his actions and his speech are characterized according to whether they proceed out of whole hugr, bold hugr, or downcast hugr. It resides in him and urges him on; thus ends Loki, when he has said his say among the gods: 'Now I have spoken that which my hugr urged me to say.' Thus also Sigurd, when he has slain the serpent: 'My hugr urged me to it.'"[105]

Our *hugr* is also the means by which we project ourselves outward. "Now and again, the soul has its knowledge directly, as we should say; at times, it has acquired it by spying out the land, and then it may chance that the enemy has seen his opponent's hugr coming toward him, whether in human form or in the shape of a beast. He dreams of wolves and is told that it is the hugrs of men he has seen."[106]

Frith and Honor

Frith is the first of three Norse-Germanic principles underlying kinship. The other two are honor and luck. Frith is not a straightforward concept, as it has different shades of meaning. *Frith* means freedom. It indicates a state of peace, goodwill, and calm. These are qualities necessary for functional kinship or community. Furthermore, frith deals with the social interactions and relationships conducive to peace. Within frith, we discover the word *friend*. It is the bond of honor that holds families and communities together.

"Frith is the mutual will, the unanimity, gentleness, loyalty, in which men live within their circle."[107] In a word, the feeling of firth is love. This is the love of kin that means unity and interconnectedness between each other. There is a oneness of soul. In other words, everyone has each other's back—a quality rare in today's society.

Honor: What does *honor* mean to you? Do you attempt to be honorable in all of your actions? These are important questions. Have you ever considered them? To the Norse-Germanic people, honor was "identical with humanity. Without honor, one cannot be a living being; losing honor, one loses the vital element that makes man a thinking and feeling creature."[108] Honor was not a standalone principle. It went hand in hand with frith. Together, they were the sum of life where happiness flowed.

"Frith and honor together constitute the soul. Of these two constituents, frith seems to lie deeper. Frith is the base of the soul; honor is all the restless matter above it. But there is no separation between them. The force of honor is the feeling of kinship, and the contents of frith is honor. So it is natural that a wound to honor is felt on one hand as an inner decline, and on the other as a paralysis of love. By the import of honor, we learn to know the character of the gladness, which kinsmen felt when they sat together by the fire warming themselves in frith."[109] In other words, the measure of a person was frith, honor, and luck (see chapter 6).

Frith and honor: Have you awakened these within your soul? In your extended family or kin, are these principles at work? If not, what can be done to make them a part of your family circle? How about coworkers? Consider getting together with them to discuss frith and honor, and then, implement these important principles within the work environment.

Nature—Heart and Nature as One

> Go to the mountains, sit by a tree, and listen with heart and
> mind; walk in the valleys with the winds caressing your soul,
> and listen with heart and mind; lie by a river with its soothing
> lullaby, and listen with heart and mind; skip a stone in childlike
> innocence across the mirror surface of a lake, and listen with

heart and mind; feel the fire of the sun on your face, and listen
with heart and mind; let the moonlight blanket you with its
beauty, and listen with heart and mind; stand and gaze at
the night sky with its star-studded tapestry, and listen with
heart and mind to the sound of angels; and let the rain cleanse
you of pain and suffering, and listen with heart and mind.
REV. DR. JC HUSFELT

"In Scandinavia, nature is peopled by powers in human shape. Up from the earth and out from the hills, elf and dwarf peer forth, a host of giants bellow from the mountains, from the sea answer Ran's daughters, those enticing and hardhearted wave maidens, with their cruel mother, and at home in the hall of the deep, sits venerable Ægir. Over the heavens go sun and moon; some indeed declare that the two drive in chariots with steeds harnessed to their carts; the sun is chased by two wolves eager to swallow its shining body. Of the sun and the moon, it is said, both that they were given and taken in marriage, and that they have left offspring."[110]

⚜

Have you ever taken the time to go out into nature, away from human encroachment, and just sat on the earth and felt the beauty and love surrounding you? Have you taken the time to see elf and dwarf peer forth from field and stone? Have you ever considered that you have no other reason than to just be part of and in partnership with nature; no smart phones or tablets, no hiking from point to point, but just you, and the Great Mother—Freyja, seeing, feeling, hearing, smelling, and even tasting the essence of the kingdom of nature?

Earth is a paradise of wonders all wrapped up in myriad colors. It is alive with a consciousness that responds to all the things that call it home. I believe in a partnership with the earth and feel at one with it. I do not believe in being superior to nature, acting as its steward, but instead acting as one with nature and in partnership with the earth in cocreating a paradisiacal state of life for all life.

When was the last time you viewed the miracle of sunrise; the wonder of sunset; the magical rise of the moon in its fullness, reminding you of the interpenetration of light within dark? Have you ever been in awe of the darkness of a new moon, knowing that all growth is born out of darkness? When are you going to awaken to the paradise spread before you—the kingdom of Óðinn as Allfather?

When I talk about Mother Nature, I'm referring not only to the earth but also to the whole of the seen and unseen universe. Mother Nature is wondrous, magical, and a miracle of creation. The universe as Mother Nature is a great concept to embrace. It expands our concern and consciousness for the well-being of all things out to the stars. This takes the religious philosophical concept of the kingdom of Óðhinn from just being earthbound out to the stars—the totality of the universe!

Having our heart and nature as one essence is essential for our well-being of body, mind, and spirit. Our heart will assist us in connecting with nature, and nature will help us be connected to our heart—a blending of both. We may metaphorically consider Yggdrasill the heart of the earth and the heart of heaven, pumping the lifeblood of creation through all things of existence.

The Heart

Wondrous and magical is the heart physically and spiritually. It is the center of our consciousness of oneness, while the brain is the center of our dualistic consciousness. Amazingly, the heart possesses its own nervous system. Additionally, the heart thinks! It is an intelligence system. In fact, the brain receives more orders from the heart than the heart receives from the brain.

Furthermore, our indigenous ancestors "understood the heart's ability to intelligently perceive and decipher the world around them, and acknowledged the limitations and reductionist nature of living in a manner in which one relies primarily on the mind.

"They went beyond the thoughts in their heads, using the heart as an organ of perception to connect with the energy fields of other organisms – not just other humans, but the earth as well – in order to fully immerse themselves in the deeper meanings embodying their thoughts."[111]

Moreover, new research has discovered that the heart has a sense of smell. Even more amazing is the hormone it secretes—oxytocin.[112] This is the bonding or love hormone that brings things together. In this bonding we experience feelings of compassion, harmony, love, and peace. In other words, the heart is the key to our awakening of radical nondualistic consciousness.

Friluftsliv

"Free air life" is the literal translation of the Norwegian word *Ffriluftsliv*. Philosophically, it means the direct experience of the natural world. This is viewed as a deep inner connection to nature and not a separation from it. It is a partnership with the land. The earth is sacred and needs to be respected and honored. It is the wise one who ventures into the wild seeking peace, solitude, and the openness to converse with the spirits of the land—and the creatures of this world.

The concept of frith was extended outward to one's natural surroundings, where the line of separation dissolved between us and nature. Honor and worshipping was conducted in nature possibly near the sacredness of waterfall, tree, or stone. Here the soul of the individual became one with the soul of nature. This was and still is the freedom, power, love, and wisdom available to all humanity.

Tree Whisperer

One of my favorite memories as a young child is of cutting down a Christmas tree. This was in the fifties in rural Maryland. My vision of wonder was centered on forging through the snow on a cold afternoon, through a magical forest of silence, with three of my great-uncles. I spent many of my days visiting with my grandmother and her brothers and sisters on their small farm. It was one uncle, Albert, who fostered and nourished in me the uncomplicated facts of life and the beauty and wisdom of the fruits and flowers of creation. He would let me help him while he tended his Concord grape vines and nurtured his pride and joys, the bright flowers with the sword-shaped leaves—gladioluses. Picking a grape and holding it between his thumb and forefinger, he once spoke these wise words to me: "Jimmy, this is the perfect color of purple; if you pick the grape when it is a lighter color, it will rob the vine of its gift. And if it is a deeper bluish purple, you will have dishonored the vine by letting the grape stay on too long."

Sherry and I and our two children continued this ancestral tree-cutting tradition for many wintry seasons. Once during a snowstorm, I had to carry our young daughter through knee-high snow, and the tree we selected turned out to be not so perfect when the snow melted off and there were few branches. Having family together choosing the perfect tree for honoring and celebration is wondrous and in the memories last for life.

The selection of which tree to cut was not fully a democratic process. It was Sherry who made the final decision. My wife is a true empath. This soul ability also takes the form of "tree speak." We would pick out a tree, and Sherry would talk to it to see if it wanted to go home with us. She would usually speak first to the tree, except for one time, Christmas of 2014. I had spotted a tree that looked perfect for us. Meanwhile, Sherry was talking to another person while I was roaming around. As she walked near the tree coming toward me, the tree spoke to her: "Hey, come here." Needless to say, she was a little taken aback. Usually she initiates the dialogue. As she put her hand on the tree, it said, "I want to go home with you. I want to go where there are hidden ones, but don't let that cat run up me."

Our magical tree stayed alive within our home for just shy of three months; one day it was still viable, and the next day, the branches were stiff as a board.

Red Paint

As we all know, blood is a life carrier. Arterial blood carries oxygen, while venous blood carries carbon dioxide from the tissues to the lungs to be exhaled. Humans and trees work in an awesome and magically wise partnership. Trees produce oxygen, which we breathe, and absorb carbon dioxide, which we exhale. This synergetic relationship needs to be seen as one of the most important spiritual-religious philosophies, resulting in a paradigm of honor, respect, and nurturing care between the human race and the earth. Adapting this philosophy alone will help return a green philosophical mindset to humanity.

Our blood is the source of all that is life giving. Blood as a mysterious spiritual power may be symbolized and exemplified by the color red. As I have noted, the yew bleeds a red-colored resin, symbolizing blood. Since time immemorial, there has been another substance symbolizing the ritualistic life-giving and regenerative magical power of blood—the earth pigment red ochre. Ochre is a natural earth clay containing hydrated iron oxide. Red ochre contains large amounts of the mineral hematite, which is a dehydrated iron oxide. Hematite's name comes from *haima*, the Greek word for blood, a reference to hematite's distinctive color.

Red paint is made from red ochre and was associated with human burials for millennium. In fact red ochre in the form of red paint dates as far back as 250,000 to 300,000 years ago! The religious and spiritual power of red paint was used to symbolize blood, life, power, fertility, renewal, and even death (and subsequently rebirth/reincarnation). Warriors would apply red ochre to their weapons imbuing them with magical powers. In a sense, it strengthened their minds.

> Moreover, we know that the most popular color for the runes themselves was red (made with red oxide of lead, minium, or most often, ochre). This was generally a magical substitute for blood (see *Egil's Saga*, chapter 44). Comparative historical linguistics gives us good evidence for the magical importance of the color red for the Germanic peoples. The Old English *teafor* is an old term for red ochre, but the word is also found in Old High German as *zouber* (magic, divination) and in Old Norse as *taufr* (talismanic magic, talisman). It seems that one of the old ways "to do magic" was "to make red [with ochre]" some symbolic object in conjunction with a transference of magical might. This technique is made very clear in the passage from *Egil's Saga* cited above.[113]

The use of red paint has long played an important part in shamanic tradition. Red paint has a protective power against intrusion from the spirit world, such as during a *blót* burning—feeding the spirits. Having had the knowledge, power, and authority to use red paint during ritual, ceremony, and healing passed on to me, I know its effect and power. Before I put a person into the stream, for bathing, I paint them with a symbol that is possibly older than the pyramids. It is exactly the same as one of the magical symbols that concluded certain runic inscriptions. Magic is alive: just listen, look, and learn.

Landvættir and Huldufólk

Landvættir are the land spirits linked with the land itself. Being in friendship/ partnership and honoring the landvættir could bring prosperity to a family in farming, hunting, and fishing. Additionally, they provided protection to the children and animals. These elemental spirits primarily dwelled in mounds/ mountains, waterfalls, groves, and areas of unusual landscape.

According to Hilda Roderick Ellis's *The Road to Hel*, there is recorded a:

> statement at the beginning of the heathen laws that men must not sail to land with grinning and gaping figureheads on their ships, but must remove them while some distance from Iceland, so that the land spirits may not be frightened by them. The idea of the land spirits as protective beings, whose friendship is a valuable one, is brought out again by the little incident in *Landnámabók*, of the lucky man called Björn who was assisted by the land spirits so that his herds increased and he prospered greatly:

> ...Men with the gift of second-sight watched all the land-spirits fol- lowing Hafr-Björn to the Þing, and Þorsteinn and Þórðr (his brothers) hunting and fishing.[114]

Iceland's National Coat of Arms portrays four landvættir who are protectors of the four quarters of Iceland. The four land guardians are: the dragon (Dreki) in the northeast, the eagle or griffin (Gammur) in the northwest, the bull (Griðungur) in the southwest, and the giant (Bergrisi) in the southeast. These guardians are ever watchful and alert for invaders. There is another word con- nected with the concept of the landvættir. The word is *landdisir* ("dísir of the land"). According to Rudolf Simek, the "*landdísir* were perhaps identical with the *dísir*, female protective goddesses, or else are related in some way to the landvættir, Icelandic protective spirits. The fact that the *landdísir* were thought to live in rocks, where they were also venerated (hence the term *landdisas- teinar*), could mean that this devotion was a form of ancestor cult and that the dead were venerated here."[115] In short, the land spirits—the elementals who are everywhere and are an embodiment of nature itself—must be respected.

⚜

Another aspect of the unseen ones are the hidden folk (hidden ones)—the *huldufólk*. These unseen ones could be referred to as the Alfar—elves or faeries. It is interesting to note that the elves could have been the male counterparts to the dísir.

As I well know, they often have contact with us humans. It is best not to offend them. When traveling to new places, it is best to acknowledge the spirits, the unseen ones, of the land, not only the huldufólk but the landvættir as well. The ceremony does not need to be extensive but from our hearts. It is important to ask permission to be in this new land, to do our spiritual work, and for health and protection while journeying through their land. Since these symbolize a gift from the unseen ones, we need to give back—a gift demands a gift. This gifting could take the form of alcohol left for them or poured on the earth, or incense/sacred herbs burned as a gift of sweet essence. Even leaving a few flowers on the ground would be a right action. Finally, a small sacrifice as a gift—pull some hair and leave it on the earth. End with thankfulness and a blessing for the well-being of all the unseen ones. In over thirty years of journeying to distant lands, my wife and I can attest to the effectiveness of this practice.

Embracing Freyja's Power of Nature

> Be aware and listen...a thought or prayer and
> then...the rustle of leaves...it is only the wind you
> think...but who sends the wind...the gods

To embrace Freyja's power of nature, consider planting a tree, such as an apple tree, to honor one of your ancestors or family members, or plant a tree as a guardian tree of your land as a honoring to the landvættir. Spend time just wandering through forests. Artur Lundkvist is one Swedish literature's greatest tree worshippers. Following a reflection on trees and forests, he writes:

In every human there is a tree, and in every tree there is a human, I feel this, the tree wanders inside a human being, and the human being is caught in the tree...I serenade the forests, the forest sea is the second sea on earth, the sea in which man wanders. The forests work in silence, fulfilling nature's mighty work; working with the winds, clean-ing the air, mitigating the climate, forming soil, preserving all our es-sentials without wearing them out.[116]

Huldufólk, or hidden ones, seem to like stone and possibly cats. Constructing a stone circle on your land would be an honoring and a sacred place of blót and meditation. The stone circle does not need to have the stones touching each other. In fact, a more sacred way is a few large stones that form a circle or oval. This is witnessed by ancient stone circles such as the Ring of Brodgar on the Orkney Islands and Avebury in England.

One way to experience a connection with Freyja is for our skin to touch the earth. Remove your shoes and walk with bare feet on the sacred earth. Sit and lie upon the earth to feel its energetic force or, even better, bare yourself to the earth. This allows us to see more clearly and feel kinship with all things near us. Everything has an intrinsic personality. Before we can talk to trees or stones, we must first listen to them. The world is our library, encoded within the stones, leaves, grass, brooks, seas, fjords, and animals—all things of Freyja's paradise. The closer we are to nature, the nearer we are to the beauty and truth of our hearts. If there is a lack of respect for nature, then there will be a lack of respect for other human beings.

⚜

An important fact to ponder:

It has now been confirmed by science that hugging trees can benefi-cially affect human health by altering vibrational frequency. In a re-cently published book by Matthew Silverstone, *Blinded by Science*, evidence confirming trees and their healthful benefits includes their effect on mental illnesses, Attention Deficit Hyperactivity Disorder (ADHD), concentration levels, reaction times, depression, and the ability to alleviate headaches.

According to countless studies cited within the book, children show extreme psychological and physiological effects in terms of im-proved health and well-being when they interact with plants. It was recorded that children function better cognitively and emotionally in green environments and have more creative play in green areas.

A large public health report studying the association between green spaces and mental health also noted that "access to nature can significantly contribute to our mental capability and well-being."

Human beings can only live outside of the laws of nature for so long before symptoms of disconnect be made manifest.[117]

⚜

Even though wisdom is the province of Óðinn, wisdom may be discovered within Freyja's realm. Wisdom does not come with age, like a fine wine. It comes through the experience of direct knowledge, our knowing. Knowledge may be discovered through books and oral teachings. But, ah, this is not wisdom. When we have a direct experience of knowledge, wisdom may be birthed within us. It is important to understand: wisdom is not to be discovered within books, ivy-covered institutions, or institutionalized theology. And it will not be discovered within human-made structures, such as a church. However, we may directly experience and discover wisdom within nature: the valleys and the mountains, the rivers and the oceans, the flight of an eagle, the croak of a frog, the sound of the rain, the crash of thunder, the path of the serpent, and the sun, moon, and stars above. Freyja's realm is the teacher and the giver of wisdom. Before it is too late, humanity must seek truth and wisdom from nature, not nature's destruction for greed and power.

In other words, we need to seek our knowledge, power, and wisdom in nature. The workings of the earth have always provided an enduring source of spiritual wisdom and knowledge. Immersing one's self in Freyja's nature under the sun, the clouds, and the stars will reveal insights and knowledge unattainable within the human-made walls of any school or institution. With their hearts firmly entrenched in nature, many masters of the past have felt that the mountains, streams, and waterfalls were the locations of true knowledge and their true selves. It was at such places where they were inspired and expanded their spiritual powers.

Training in nature, far away from the irritations and distractions of modern life, will help us uncover the body-mind that is so important in awakening. This is not the body and mind of dualistic thinking, but body/mind—the actual experience and being of the oneness of life. With the sky overhead and the earth beneath our feet, we may experience what the Norse of old felt—nature as school. But remember that nature and the earth are unforgiving of one's unhealthy ego and stupidity. Common sense as well as preparation is indispensable in nature's wildness. Many people lack directional sense, and even if you do have a good sense of direction, a compass, a map, and the knowledge of how to use them are essential. If you choose to go alone into a wilderness area, it is best to let someone know where you are going and your expected time of return. Water, a knife, matches or lighter, and a day pack with a change of clothes, extra socks, and some fruit and trail mix are a good idea if you are planning on spending the day out in nature; in addition, be informed of the local weather conditions. One further point, the preceding is of utmost importance as the power to survive is to be found within ourselves. In other words, a smart phone may be included with your items, but do not totally be dependent on it. Look to yourself not technology.

Once you are in nature, there are many methods that will help you develop and strengthen your spirit and wisdom. I will suggest a few basic exercises that I have used with my students:

❖ Listen, Look, Learn, and Know:
  A meditative walk using all of your senses except your eyes, which can switch from half closed to fully closed to fully open. Our eyes happen to be one of the prime gateways for spiritual afflictions or attachments to occur in our mind. The majority of people's eyes normally see, and what they see they attach to, thus arresting the mind and allowing desires, judgments, fears, and many other mind afflictions to arise.

  Our goal is to listen and see with our hearts as well as with our metaphoric third eyes, or intuitive eyes, which are above our physical eyes and centered in our foreheads, and connect us with the pituitary and pineal glands in the brain.

  We have only explored our eyes, but each of our senses may be deemed the source of our passions—things that disturb the tranquility of our mind. Think about this and then develop an experiential exercise based on this knowledge to help you develop your megin.

❖ A quest in nature would be another tool to help you in discovering self-knowledge. This involves nothing more than just sitting or, a little harder, standing in one spot for two or more hours. This means just being with ourselves with the sky and the earth as witnesses without moving or doing anything. Sitting against the base of a tree would be very enlightening, as the tree has its roots in the earth and its branches reaching toward the sky, symbolizing the unity of and connection between sky and earth.

Listen to the tree; then commune with it. Sit in silence for a period of time. After your mind is calm and without mind chatter, you may begin visualizing and feeling your energy within your spine merging with the tree's energy. Practice moving this merged energy up both you and the tree and then descending down your spine and within the tree's trunk.

After practicing the above for a few weeks, a more advanced exercise involves standing with your back and full body against an elder (older) tree. First, ask permission of the tree for you to work with its body and soul. If permission is granted, first hug the tree for a few minutes then stand with your back and full body against the tree. Begin slow breathing while maintain the awareness of all sensory input. Slowly close your eyes. After a few seconds begin visualizing a light in the center of your brain (pineal gland); keep being aware of all of your senses. Slowly descend this light down your spine until it merges with the base of your spine (sacrum and coccyx). There are nine segments of the sacrum (5) and coccyx (4). Nine is the sacred number of humans. The pineal gland is our potential pine cone of light. When it awakens, the sacred number becomes ten[118]—the sacred number of divine human beings.

Maintain this column of light flowing from your pineal to your sacrum and coccyx. This flow is both descending and ascending. Listen and feel the soul of the tree. Let it feel your soul. After a period of time let your body and soul merge with the trees body and soul. Feel, and be, the essence of the tree and yourself as one. However, always keep a ten percent awareness of your separate self. After a period of time, let your internal column of light descend through your feet and down through the roots of the tree and then ascend this sacred light up from the roots of the tree through you and continuing up to the very top of the tree. Be one with all things. Maintain this interconnectedness for a period of time. When ready feel your body and soul physically separating from the tree. Be aware of all of your senses. Slowly open your eyes and observe your surroundings. As a completion, thank and bless the tree, its body and soul. Kiss it and give a gift back to it. This gifting may be as simple as some of your hair placed on the trunk of the tree or sacred ale poured on the trunk and around its base. Keep this memory alive within your heart and mind.

❖ Finally, be respectful of all things (e.g., do not litter and give thanks when you leave for your safety and all that you have learned and experienced).

Freyja's Garden Paradise of Love:
Oneness with Nature

❖ Acknowledge and believe that all things, including nature, have a consciousness and are alive and responsive.

❖ Spend consistent alone time just being with nature, not in a separate way but as a part of nature.

❖ See and acknowledge the beauty of nature and its children (creatures).

❖ Listen to a tree and converse with it.

❖ Kiss trees, flowers, plants and so-forth.

❖ Talk to the winds and the winds will talk back.

❖ See the oneness and beauty of even the smallest creatures of earth.

❖ Walk softly over the earth and consciously harm no things.

❖ Have pets if possible.

❖ Let your yard grow naturally; do not use chemicals on it and do not make it a miniature golf course.

❖ Before cutting trees (only if necessary) or picking fruit off the vine, ask permission and give blessings.

❖ Have as many plants and flowers as possible in your living space.

❖ Garden with loving care.

❖ If possible, have a vegetable and/or herb garden.

❖ Eat organically and pressure society to make organically grown food affordable for all people.
❖ Eat locally grown or raised food as often as possible.
❖ Walk often and be with nature.
❖ Bless the overcast sky as well as the clear, blue sky; bless the sun and the moon; bless the wind and the rain.
❖ Spend time with your family in nature.
❖ Bless nature and its importance to all daily.
❖ Increase the time that you normally spend outdoors.
❖ Walk barefoot on the earth.
❖ Forgo a hat or umbrella during rain and experience Þórr's sweat and tears on your head—no rain, no rainbows.
❖ Listen, look, and learn from nature.
❖ Be one with the ocean and the sea; sit by a fjord and experience the power and wonder.
❖ These are just a few guidelines—what others can you add?

Our modern age of sterility is not healthy for us. This separation mentality is dysfunctional and unhealthy. Our bodies need bacteria. Their presence helps our systems stay healthy and balanced. So go outside, be in close relationship with Freyja's paradise, and get dirty!

Fylgja

Fylgja, a following spirit or someone who accompanies, may be considered a person's guardian spirit. It is one of our connections between spirit and matter. Metaphorically, as a follower, our guardian has our back. As it also accompanies us, it may be sent to retrieve knowledge. Additionally, "The idea of the 'spirit' or 'external soul' leaving the body, either in human or animal form, to travel vast distances or to fight the spirits of others in similar form, is one that occurs frequently in Norse tradition."[119] This spirit combat is a common motif in shamanism with encounters in the otherworld between rival shamans. The ability to accomplish these types of feats comes from the power of a strong mind—in other words, luck. A guardian spirit may be in animal or human, usually female, form and "is the active, invisible companion which attends the owner in his waking state."[120]

The female form of the fylgja survives the physical death of a person, and is a "supernatural woman guardian, attached to one particular family, who at the death of the man she attends passes on to one of his descendants."[121] These female guardians are connected to the female psychopomps—*valkyrjar*—and the concept of rebirth.

Similar to the fylgja is the *hamr*. This is our birth guardian, not separate but a part of us. Many times, we may observe with intuitive sight the birth guardian etched on a person's face and the movement of their body. In other words, a person, "who really appeared as wolf, as bear, as ox, as eagle, had the character-marks of wolf, bear, ox, or eagle in him always. His luck was of such a sort as to imply an essential relationship between him and his beast; he used its strength, its courage, its wildness, its craft, its power of divination, and its power of tracking, also in daylight and in his own body."[122] Do you know your birth guardian? If so, how has it helped you through the struggles of life?

In addition to fylgja and hamr, we have the concept of *hamingja*—soul connected with luck. (I discuss both hamingja and luck in the next chapter on Þórr.)

Death and Rebirth

When you accept life, you accept death
One of the keys to life.
How well will you die?

Death has such a stigma in American culture and society, which has resulted in life being preserved beyond the point of any quality of existence. The fear of death rules many of our medical decisions—length of life trumps quality of life e.g. chemotherapy instead of natural alternative therapies. Most people can't let go because there is little belief or recognition that we are each divine and human, meaning our souls are eternal and will once again return to the earth (through reincarnation), where we will continue our soul's evolution. Life is precious to me, but I know there will come a time when I need to embrace the courage to let go of this earthly existence and thus pass over with love, power, and dignity back to the heavenly realms.

I purposely use the phrase "passing over" instead of "dying" or "passing away" as a strong statement of life as eternal and not finite. It is not an ending, not extinction, but a beginning. "The word *death* has become indelibly associated in Western minds with the belief in the finality of extinction...The time has come to drop the word from our vocabulary altogether, and from our minds. Until this is done, belief will continue that life itself can die, hence an ever-increasing tendency to a completely materialistic outlook."[123]

A person who symbolically faces his or her death experiences rebirth. It is an initiation of life through symbolic death. By experiencing symbolic death, the fear of physical death has less of a hold on us. Additionally, death cannot fetter us when we believe in immortality. Physical death is nothing more than the ending of an old way of being and the beginning of the new. As an initiation, it could be a vow to live your life in the ways of the Norse ancestors, a commitment to frith, honor, and luck and to your family and kin.

Bathing—the Initiatory Rite of Death and Rebirth

Ritualistic immersion in running water (a stream or river) or the ocean is one of the oldest forms of symbolic death and rebirth and the sacrifice of self to self. It is frightening but necessary. We need to physically and symbolically die to the old to be born again. It doesn't bring membership into an earthly or religious institution. It is the beginning of an awakening to the truth—of the world and one's authentic self.

Going bathing will help a person release the stress and hurt that comes from living in today's chaotic and fear-filled world. Quite possibly, it may also be a preventative for cancer and Alzheimer's.[124]

After the initiation, there are multiple reasons for a person to revisit a stream and bathe. Bathing will increase our megin and our inner heat. The stream will also help release anger, guilt, resentment, fear, and uncertainty, as well as the other emotional baggage that we carry and seemingly refuse to release. In addition, I use it as a method of healing others.

Bathing, as a sacrifice of self to self, is not easy, especially when you consider that the training period is during the winter. Northern winters can be extremely brutal, cold, and snowy. Many times I had to break through the ice to bathe. One time, I even wondered if I would make it back to my car alive as I trudged through the thigh-high snow with no feeling in my legs. But the experience is awesome. Even after countless bathings I still feel a little trepidation and fear each time.

Imagine standing nude before first light on the edge of a flowing river while listening to the sounds of the rushing waters as if they are the sounds of the thundering wagon of Þórr. And further imagine your bare feet on the sacred ground of the earth (sometimes snow-covered), your naked body feeling the winds of the earth, while your uncovered head and eyes observe the dimming night sky—one embedded with hundreds of sparkling jewels. And then you voice prayers to Freyja, the spirits of the land, and Óðinn before entering alone and submerging yourself. When I enter the river, with my first step, there is an explosion of my senses and the illusion of dualistic reality dissolves into a oneness of truth. With my first squatting submersion, I die once again, only to be reborn as I explode straight up out of the water, into the air with a primal scream escaping from my lips. And for a split second, my mind shifts into the realization that I must do this three more times.

After the fourth submersion, as I shoot up out of the waters, my spirit song erupts from the inner core of my soul. How long I remain in the freezing waters is always a mystery. The siren song is always to stay in the power—megin—to stay in the true oneness of life where human worries and fears do not exist: it is only you and the mystery of regin—divine power.

It is impossible for me to bathe everyone reading this book. However, with a few precautions, you may visit a stream or ocean to experience the rebirthing power of bathing. Most importantly, you will need someone to accompany you to witness your rebirth and for your safety. In fact, you could both bathe, one at a time. This practice is too dangerous to do alone.

Before the morning of bathing, it is a good idea to purchase a new set of Viking era clothing. You would dress in this clothing after bathing. Bathing is done in the nude and pre–first light—not predawn but pre–first light. This is approximately one hour before sunrise. A gift from the otherworld of spirit calls for a gift from us. A blessing, words of power and prayer, and a gifting needs to be done before we enter the waters and after we leave. A gifting of ale may be poured upon the waters. Enter the water facing downstream or north if in the sea, and completely submerge yourself three times. Let any sounds come out as an expression of your megin. Exit the waters and bask in the new you as you put on your new clothes. Sit quietly for a period of time, merging with your natural surroundings. Just before you depart, bless Freyja, Freyr, Njörðr, Þórr, Óðinn, spirits of the land, and all the unseen ones. Leave in the joy and peace of firth.

Valkyrjar

When the discussion turns to battle and death, our minds generate images of the Valkyrjar (Old Norse "those who choose the slain"). The feeling of their power and the emotion they invoke may be best exemplified by Richard Wagner's "Ride of the Valkyries." The power of these female psychopomps is not limited to the battlefield but includes their power to protect heroes and to teach magical lore.

Valkyrjar are best known as being connected with Óðinn, but there seems to also be a link between Freyja and them. In "Grímnismál," "We are told that Freyja shares with Othin the power to 'choose' the slain, and that they share with her, her hall, Fólkvangr." It's been put forward that Fólkvangr "is merely a synonym, like Valhöll, for the field of battle,"[125] which would suggest "that Freyja is the true Valkyrie, welcoming the dead with wine within the house of the gods."[126]

Additionally, "the Valkyrjar are not clearly distinguishable from other minor feminine deities such as the Dísir or the Nornar. All are considered to represent different manifestations of a belief in a number of female supernatural beings. In her mythological role as the chooser of half of the fallen warriors for her death realm Fólkvangr, the goddess Freyja, however, emerges as the mythological role model for the Valkyrjar and the Dísir."[127] If we delve into both Gods:

Óðinn and Freyja, the concept of guidance is expressed through their role as the divine representatives most engaged in interfering in the matters of man. Even though the Old Norse gods were generally described as influential powers, it is predominantly Óðinn and Freyja who seem to have been regarded as powers, specifically manipulating the fate and destiny of individuals or groups. The special role of Óðinn and Freyja is indicated by the fact that both are described as ruling their own death realm and that only they are in possession of the magic art of *seiðr*, enabling them to foresee and affect the future. Most apparently, however, it is expressed through their association with helping spirits or servants who extend the effect of their agency into the world of man.

The Valkyrjar/Dísir directly relate to the conception of Óðinn and Freyja as influential Gods. ... Especially in the context of heroic poetry, they are described as directly influencing or deciding an individual's fate. The majority of the evidence relates to their role of choosing the warriors on the battlefield, and thereby influencing the outcome of a battle. Especially as regards the Dísir and the Nornar, which both are related to the concept of the Valkyrjar, their agency seems to have been regarded as more universal, affecting among others the destiny of female individuals.[128]

Considering the preceding and even though the Valkyrjar are traditionally connected with Óðinn, I choose to discuss them in this chapter due to the next section and true story. One final point to ponder: could Óðinn and Freyja respectively symbolize the absolute and relative aspects of creation?

Valkyrjar and the Moment of Death

What happens the moment we die? Do we still maintain a form of consciousness? Is there a bright light and/or a long tunnel? To the second question, I answer yes, and to the third question, I answer no. Of course, to an extent, these are unanswerable spiritual and religious mysteries. I pose one more question: Are our guides at death female in appearance? I have a knowing, not 100 percent but close to it, that the answer is yes.

Of the many cultures separate from the Norse-Germanic lands, few have female psychopomps such as the Valkyrjar. Rome had Mercury, Hermes was the Greek psychopomp, Anubis the Egyptian, and of course, the Grim Reaper—all seemingly male. Even the Grim Reaper gives the indication of being male, as depicted in the movie *The Seventh Seal* where he plays chess against a knight for his soul. The Nordic psychopomps were primarily female, the Valkyrjar, even though Freyja and Óðinn would also sometimes act as psychopomps for the Norse. In Finnish folklore we discover a "female guardian at death's door." "In the classic epic poem *Tuonelanmatka*, the shamanic hero Väinämöinen makes a journey to a Finnic land of the dead in pursuit of magic items. He is greeted at the river border of the land by Death's daughter (*Tuonen tytär*), who recognizes him as a living man and attempts to imprison him there. Väinämöinen escapes, however, in the shape of a serpent. The image of a female guardian at death's door finds parallels in Scandinavian myths of Hel."[129] I believe that this poem and other Scandinavian mythologies of death and the lore of female psychopomps are tapping into ancient, primordial knowledge. How do I know? My knowing comes from an experience in 2000 CE.

It was September; we were returning from a spiritual journey to Hawaii and were stopping over in Seattle to spend a few days with one of our apprentices and her family. After a few enjoyable days, we were headed back to SeaTac airport, outside of Tacoma, on a four-lane highway divided by grassy median. Our apprentice Jane was driving with my wife in the passenger seat, and I was in the back attempting to nap. With eyes closed all I heard was "All no." With that, my eyes flew open as I saw a car settle on its wheels on the median. "Stop," I yelled as I jumped out and hobbled across the highway to the car. Later, I was told that I did some type of arm motion as I went across the highway that seemed to slow time. They also related that the car had rolled side over side numerous times before it came to rest upright on its wheels. Jane said that she saw the driver's head violently whipping around.

As I approached the vehicle, I could see that there were two Native American men unconscious. Once by the car, I knew the passenger was injured but not dying. The driver was another story. He was dying; his soul was leaving him. When I had broken the sensory separation between this world and the otherworld, I did not know, but the otherworld and this world were one and the same at that moment. This was similar to the feeling and knowing I had during the descending spirit exorcism.

In an attempt to keep him from dying, I put my hands on him and a spirit song sprang from my lips. This was not my usual song; this one I had never sung before. When you are in this timeless space, you still have a conscious awareness. It is not a trance state but one of full awareness, total focus, and intent with a minimum of mind talk. Time had no meaning as my awareness shifted to the other side of the car where a woman, definitely Native American, was walking back and forth while looking at me. It is difficult to put into words: her facial expression and intense focus was on me, not the two in the car. I thought, *She must be pissed that a white guy is healing with a Northwest Coast spirit song.* Then my focus went back on the driver. Again, time was lost to me, until the driver opened his eyes turned, looked at me, and said, "Native..."

I replied, "No." He turned his head back and closed his eyes. I then knew that his soul was back and he was not dying. With that, I left, as I heard the sounds of an ambulance coming, and in that moment, I had a fleeting thought, *Where was the native woman?* She had disappeared.

In hindsight, I realize that no other cars had stopped to help. This in itself was very unusual, as accidents seem to draw humans like bees to honey.

The irony at the time was that I never gave the native woman's disappearance any further consideration. It was only years later, when out of the clear blue the thought came into my mind: *She was a spirit psychopomp to assist the native man passing over. And however the sisters weave the threads, I had prevented it.* When this finally happened, I asked both my wife and Jane about the woman; they didn't see her but thought that possibly there could have been.

So is the guide that helps us pass over a female? Does she appear as one of our own race? Did the Vikings have it right all along and the other cultures that have gotten more press time and scholarly focus, such as the Egyptians, metaphorically missed the boat? If we use common sense, a woman births us and delivers us into our earthly existence. Why would a female not assist us in departing?

Þórr
Power of Mind

CHAPTER 6

Þórr

Þórr is an inspiration, a guiding light that may lighten our darkness, just as his hammer's lightning streaks through the sky. His rain fertilizes the earth, just as our own tears may heal us and fertilize the barren parts of our wounded selves. Þórr is the son of the earth. He is Þórr Fjörgynsson: Þórr "Son of Life's Struggles." In other words, the Norse metaphorically referred to the earth as "life struggle." At various times, our journeys through life are struggles. This is Þórr's realm, the earth and the sky. And just as light has a function, so does Þórr. One of his functions is to help us through life's struggles. Þórr has our back!

Þórr may be viewed as the personification of the earth and sky. He is also the personification of gravity. His realm is Þrúðvangr (Old Norse for "power field") and his hall is called Bilskirnir (Old Norse for "lightning crack"). Sif is his wife and his one daughter is Þrúðr (powerful). His two sons are Móði (ON, "angry one") and Magni (ON, "the strong one"). According to Vilhelm Gronbech, both sons are "his powerful courage and resolution."[130] Our children are extensions of ourselves, even though they are intrinsically unique individuals. So it is with the children of Þórr—anger, strength, power, powerful courage, and resolution (possibly a resolute heart) may help us in understanding and overcoming our struggles of life.

Just like Óðinn, we must not put limits on Þórr or squeeze him into a box. Þórr, on one hand, is a warrior god, god of thunder. On the other hand, he is a sky god and god of fertilization. As the thunder god, he is the embodiment of intention. This intention is projected through his hammer, Mjǫllnir. Þórr's stone hammer is the symbol of the thunderbolt, which is of Hyperborean origin. This represents intention (strong mind) through directed and focused action (healthy body). Additionally, Mjǫllnir (crusher, miller) is "the pulverizing force that destroys as well as creates."[131]

Additionally, just as our eyes are the portals to our souls, we discover that Þórr is the fierce-eyed one reflecting his anger toward the ones who destroy and cause chaos. Just as the thunder roars against injustice and lightning streaks thru the sky, Þórr rides his brazen wagon through the heavens, completely surrounded by the glistening sparks flying from the hoofs of his two goats: Tanngniostr (tooth cracker) and Tanngrisnr (tooth gnasher). (These names of Þórr's goats were most likely made up by Snorri and not based on ancient knowledge.)

Thunder, Þórr's voice, gives us insight into the power of vocal vibration. This power of vibration results in a strong heart, mind, and voice. Thunder is the power of Þórr's voice. Everything is energy, all vibration. To bring about change and/or transformation, we need intention and the interaction of body, mind, and voice—the vibrational power of our soul. And sometimes just as Þórr's rain fertilizes the earth, our tears need to purify our heart.

Every moment, our words need to be based on truth, not lies. Our words need to be in congruence with our heart, not our unhealthy ego. Every word we speak needs to reflect a powerful, loving, and compassionate heart. This is everyday speak, but what about mystical words? This is where chanting comes into play as well as the Norse *galdr*—formulaic incantations.

Thunder and lightning were not only a physical sound and visual experience of the sky's wonders, which foretold the birth of life-giving rains, but they were also the voice of Þórr and his hammer streaking across the sky. Thunder and lightning were both spirit and matter as one. Then there is the question of fire (spirit) and matter. If we say they are kept separate, "we boldly disregard the fact that certain stones strike off sparks and certain kinds of wood produce fire when rubbed. Primitive men arrange the facts in another pattern, saying that fire belongs to the nature or soul of tree and stone—the sparks are conceived and begotten by the fire drill; consequently there is an innate kinship between stones and trees on the one hand and the fire that comes down from the heavens on the other."[132]

Þórr Speaks

Knowing one of my past incarnations, I wanted and needed to celebrate my sixtieth birthday in Greece, specifically in Delphi and on the field of battle where defeat was a victory—Thermopylae. It was a bittersweet birthday. For my seventieth, I thought that I needed to go to Israel. I even told some of our students to prepare to travel to Israel in 2016.

During the summer of 2013, I was preparing for our annual journeys to Norway and Iceland and hadn't thought much about the Israel journey for possibly a year or more. I had walked out into our kitchen to speak to Sherry when for no logical reason at all, the thought came into my mind, *Maybe Israel is not the place for my seventieth*, and with that thought, thunder erupted even though there were clear skies. I said, "Þórr has spoken." I told Sherry what thought was in my mind when the thunder erupted, and she agreed: we will not be journeying to Israel for my seventieth.

This story demonstrates the essence of Þórr. Þórr represents a force of nature, but that force of nature is tied into the soul essence of Þórr, as he is a sentient energetic being. Þórr is a reality of the otherworld and interacts with this world through various forces of nature. This personal experience also points us to the fact that Þórr symbolizes the mind. Where Óðinn is spirit, Þórr is mind. Furthermore, this episode reinforces and teaches us a few truths. One of these is radical nonduality. I was not in a trance state or conducting any type of spiritual/religious activity. It was simply a very common and mundane moment. But the sacred is always blended with our mundane world. At any moment, the sacred may speak to us in its language. Many times, this is through nature. Moses wasn't locked away within a temple that separated him from nature but out in the mountains when he came upon the burning bush. Jesus had his vision and heard the divine voice while bathing predawn in a flowing river. In the case of Þórr, it was thunder that I heard. There are no coincidences. The thunder didn't occur during a storm but out of the blue, with no explainable reason.

Additionally, my mind was not chattering but still. Chatter is the mind talk that focuses our attention out of the moment to the past, future, or the disruptive influence of social media. Focusing on a smartphone disturbs the tranquility of our minds. If my mind had not been still, the thought that came out of the clear blue would not have popped into my mind and Þórr would not have responded in affirmation. It seems I do not need to travel to Israel anytime soon. We must trust ourselves and the otherworld. We must not carry any doubt. An interesting question to ponder. Where did the thought originate—from Þórr or me? Or both?

A third teaching is divine consciousness. As with the Visitation, divine consciousness interpenetrates all things. Þórr heard and responded to my thought, knowing what I did not know about the future. The future is not set but only a potential based on all the interconnected threads weaved by the Norns. If we are aware, awake, and mindful, the otherworld may guide us and provide the proper path when needed.

And the last revelation: we are never alone.

⚜

"Don't explain, and don't complain!" These wise words were told to my wife and me by a friend of ours, a Zen Roshi. It also seems that Þórr embraced this advice. He did little explaining about his actions, a trait which is uncommon today. And what about complaining? Þórr is known for his ability to accept pain without complaint. As the Son of Life's Struggles, pain is not just physical. It includes emotional, mental, and spiritual pain, which encompasses all of life's struggles. Accepting pain without complaint is behavior worthy of us all embodying.

Furthermore, Þórr is known for his strength and generosity. These are worthwhile qualities to incorporate in our lives. Þórr does not command us to be strong and generous. He is a guide and role model in life, which helps us acquire these qualities of love and power.

Son of Life's Struggle

Þórr's identity as a being connected with the struggles of life generates an otherworldly focus of compassion and support. I do not know of any other cultures whose deities' primary attribute is helping us overcome our struggles. For many of us, our physical birthing was a struggle—just ask your mother. As we develop and grow, there are the joys of life but also the struggles. For some of us, our struggles are few, and for others, many. Few or many, we still need help in making peace with or overcoming our lives' difficulties. First off, we are not alone in facing life—Þórr has our backs.

Got Our Backs

"I've got your back" is an expression of assurance that someone is protecting, supporting, and looking out for you. Such an expression reflects the Norse concept of kinship, especially when it concerns the essential qualities of frith (peace, stability, and security) and honor. Þórr has our backs. Even though he symbolizes the destructive force of storms, Þórr is the protective power against the evil acts people commit against others, including nature and all violence in general.

Strong, Powerful Mind

A strong and powerful mind is an essential attribute to assisting us in overcoming and making peace with our struggles in life. I view life as a struggle not life as suffering. A life of struggle may include suffering, but the totality of life is struggle not suffering. A philosophical shift from a worldview of suffering to struggle has a great positive effect on our hearts and minds. We are not suffering beings but struggling beings.

Furthermore, struggle is not an adverse state of being and is much better than a static, lackluster life. A lack of adventure and materialism are the providence of sheep—follow society; follow the leader. Contrary to this, a person, let's call them a wolf, forges an adventurous path in life that reflects his or her authentic self and open heart. The wolf believes in community and kinship and the qualities of frith, honor, and luck.

With a strong mind, we do not remain silent when we need to speak or stay seated when we need to stand or stay static when we need to move (with intent and directed action). In all acts, our heart is in unity with our mind.

In other words, a strong and powerful mind has a consciousness of radical nonduality—the interpenetration of spirit and matter. Our consciousness immediately feels the soul of the stone when we grasp it. Search "inanimate" on Google and the result is: "not alive, especially not in the manner of animals and humans; inanimate objects like stones."

The majority of the time, a strong mind remains in the present moment while a dualistic or weak mind is filled with mind chatter, usually based on the past or future, which is a symptom of an unhealthy ego. A chattering mind misses the beauty of nature and of life and misses the sensory treasures—the fragrant smells of nature, the feelings of rain falling on our heads, the savory taste of the morning dew, and the radiant beauty of the mountains and the sea. The chattering, dualistic mind constantly moves to external objects and attaches with judgments of their unhealthy ego. A strong mind is immovable; there are not attachments based on an unresolved past, only the sensory power of the present moment.

Where is your mind at this moment? You may spend an hour a day meditating or in prayer. But where is your mind the rest of the time? This is where true power resides—in the present moment, not in a few hours of prayer or meditation a week. Every moment is the choice—a strong mind or a weak chattering one. People that speak a lot with little to say usually have a chattering mind. Both the voice and mind are seldom silent. They don't realize that there is power in silence and listening.

From a different perspective, "we encounter the soul as *mód*, as the Anglo-Saxons have it. A man's mod is his mind, the will and strength of him, the long-remembering, that which keeps both injury and friendship alive in the foreground of his consciousness, and the boldness, which will not suffer will and memory to consume each other in indecision."[133] For further consideration, *mód* denotes not only mind but also heart, spirit, courage, pride, and anger. In other words, mód has the aspect of courage (strong mind), but it also indicates pride and anger (a weak mind). If we consider anger, there are two sides to it: one is functional, and the other is dysfunctional.

Anger

Although thoughtful and friendly in nature, Þórr is quick to anger, with a willingness to meet all challenges no matter how dangerous. Is this quality of Þórr dysfunctional, or is it functional? Immediately, the expected response concerning anger is that it's dysfunctional—anger is bad. This leads many people to suppress a natural primate reaction of our hindbrain (reptilian). Our brain is a "triune brain" composed of the hindbrain, paleomammalian brain, and our present human neomammalian brain. The hindbrain is the oldest and composed of the spinal cord, the medulla oblongata, the pons, and the cerebellum. Our reptilian brain is in charge of our basic instincts and issues of survival, dominance, mating, respiration, and heartbeat. Sometimes anger equates survival.

Yes, our anger may be dysfunctional, but when we suppress and not express our anger, it may turn into its most dysfunctional and destructive aspect—wrath and revenge. Anger based on our unhealthy ego is detrimental to our spirit and inner power. It will disturb the tranquility of our minds in the moment and, when suppressed, results in an unconscious, ongoing eroding of our peacefulness and decreases the power of our mind.

When dysfunctional anger arises, it separates and blinds us to our inner source of love and then binds our heart with discord. Everyone gets angry and everyone has been hurt. But to keep this hurt and anger alive and fresh is to live a life of bitterness and pain.

The other aspect of anger is functional. It is not destructive to our mind. This is the anger connected with injustice and restoring order from chaos. This anger once expressed is then let go. This is the anger of Þórr. It is not a coincidence that Þórr is pictured and described with fiery eyes, a red bread, and long, wild, red hair—like fire. He was known to be hot-tempered, a trait he often vented on giants. It is interesting to note that in esoteric Buddhism, there is a deity whose face is contorted in anger—the anger to destroy obstacles to awakening. This is Fudō Myō-ō. He is typically surrounded by flames of fire representing the purification of the mind by the burning away of all material desires and the passions of the mind. His anger is compassionate in the manner that it wakes people out of their mundane, materialistic sleep. Could Þórr be similar to these aspects of Fudō Myō-ō?

Connected with both types of anger is the concept of the beast within. This is explained in the next chapter. Briefly, beastly anger generates great energy. This type of energy may be utilized for constructive or destructive actions.

Ascetic Training

Life happens and we struggle through various life circumstances. Through some of our struggles, we may suffer. But in our suffering, we may become more empathic and compassionate. A seed may struggle through the earth's soil to reach the light, but there is no suffering. Struggle does not have to include suffering. We are not born to suffer; we are born in original divinity with a consciousness of radical nonduality. Both of these go into the recesses of our conscious, but they are always there. What takes their place? A consciousness of duality and separation. Herein lies our struggle and possible suffering. But we are not suffering beings, just as we are not sinful ones.

Many times our suffering is due to attachment within our minds and is connected with earthly desires. Detachment is one method to counter suffering. However, they may be aspects of life where you choose not to detach. My family is one of those. A loss of one of them would cause me to suffer deeply and greatly, to the core of my soul. This is a conscious choice not to detach and thus to potentially suffer. Like I said before, life will happen, and we will suffer in some form. But how about being proactive? Let's suffer under our own terms, which I call conscious suffering and is more commonly known as indigenous ascetic training.

Throughout the greater part of my adult life, I have accepted and embraced conscious suffering through my ascetic spiritual training. Submerging at least four times in an isolated tree-lined ice-covered stream in subzero temperatures at predawn has been one of my conscious choices of suffering. On the other hand, it was pure and soul evolving but fearful and difficult.

There are other lessons from conscious suffering, such as a knowing within our hearts and minds about compassion—an appreciation of other people's suffering. This makes us more connected to others, rather than separate from them. Another aspect is that it teaches us to be in the moment, to be present. It teaches us about conscious attention, about being aware of where we are focusing our attention. The focus of our attention receives our energy, but few of us are ever aware of the moment and the awareness of self and others.

I constantly ask our students: Where is your mind? What is it focused on? Gurus, self-help authors, and spiritual workshop teacher's talk about being present, being in the moment, but it's only taught intellectually, possibly with a few structured cozy, (nonthreatening) indoor exercises thrown in along with the lecture. But can that really teach us how to be present in the moment, without our minds chattering?

On the other hand, nature is the source for a strong and powerful mind. Stripping down to bare skin while standing alongside a rushing river at predawn puts you totally in the moment, totally aware. There is no past or future, no mind chatter except the reality of the present moment, a moment that is alive with your senses—an awareness of self and other. This is the key to adapting to a pattern within ourselves of being in the moment, being present and aware. This is conscious suffering—a suffering that steels the spirit and brightens the soul.

Ascetic training such as this affects the body as well as the mind. This type of conscious suffering helps with fear. Fear may be triggered by the mind, but the body responds immediately—heart rate increases, the breath may be held, muscles tense, etc. If you can control your mind, you can control your body; if you control your body, your mind responds. And this type of conscious suffering teaches us how to relax under stressful conditions, which can only lead to less fear in our lives—and with less fear, we experience more love and more connection with all other things. This type of body/mind presence and awareness cannot occur within the confines of a building or a church, only out in nature.

> Jesus of the gospels understood the meaning of conscious suffering in relation to sustained awareness of self and world. What we find...is that Jesus taught his disciples a deal more than the mere fact of messiahship; there is real teaching going on behind the scenes, a teaching which only barely makes its way into the synoptic gospels. And this teaching is about "awareness" and "presence" and "conscious suffering" and "levels of consciousness" in relation to "thought" and "emotion."[134]

Without conscious suffering, there is no true knowing of compassion. Compassion may be viewed as a result of our struggles to the light embodied in our suffering through hard spirit training internally and externally, which forges our sword of compassion.

How can we be spiritually compassionate and mentally powerful if we have never struggled and suffered in our quest to elevate our soul's light? Compassion, without our own personal experience, is just a word bandied about in a smug, elitist way.

Ascetic training is a ritualized activity of body and mind. Each time, the experience is different. It is not a sterile, repetitive, indoor ritual such as the Catholic Church's brainwashing Mass. In nature, even repetitive ritual actions are different each time. The more the body is involved in a natural setting, the greater effect on both body and mind. In other words, the result is a mindful body and an embodied mind.

Fear

Fear is a reality of human existence. In a few instances, it may help us in life by waking us out of a complacent stupor. On the other hand, our fight-or-flight mechanism helps us deal effectively with fear that is connected with any life-and-death situation. But there is another category of fear. This fear is by far the most damaging to us. It is our worst enemy. It is insidious. Daily, it steals a part of our soul. It is the fear that separates—the fear of the unknown.

The fear of the unknown is the fear of death as well as a fear of life, which creates a sense of powerlessness within us. This may lead to dysfunctional behaviors that give rise to an illusionary impression of power. Fear-based belief systems thrive in a cultural environment such as ours. Terrorism is ever present in people's minds, and this fear drives people to accept the erosion of their freedoms and to accept an unjust, religious, greed-based war. This type of fear enlarges people's unhealthy egos, as their minds need a secure sense of power.

Fear is the opposite of divine love. It will keep us from our bliss and an opened heart. We see the world as a dangerous place, not Freyja's earthly paradise. Fear in this sense generates greed and the desire for materialistic accumulation. It is the breeding ground for external power and the abuses that go with that power. It is the curse but also the salvation of humanity, as it has the potential to wake us out of the illusionary sleep of separation. When we let go of fear, we let go of separation; the veil is lifted, and we see and know oneness of self and others. Our inner light has evolved.

In a culture and society ruled by fear, we must access the inner core of our strength—our hearts, which will help us bring our fears out of the darkness and into the light. This transformational power, which we all have within us, fosters the courage for us to face fear. Confronting our fears, we are then able to let go of some, transform others, and finally make peace with the fears that we can't let go of or transform. In other words, firth (peace, goodwill, and calm) is a part of our soul.

It's normal and human to have fear—just never let it inhibit your life, keep you separate, or keep you from the joy of living. To conquer fear is to triumph over death. So what fears do you still harbor? Which ones can be released? The ones not released, which ones can be detached from? One further question: is the world a fearful or a loving place? Please ponder this question and see if your initial answer changes.

Courage and a Fearless Mind and Spirit

Courage is a jewel within our hearts. In life, all sorts of problems will arise to challenge our frith and honor. Courage is the vehicle to face and overcome these challenges of our soul's growth and evolution.

It takes courage to speak our truth and be who we are, even in the presence of others who want us to be something that we are not. It is courage of the heart and mind that lets us endure in the face of overwhelming sorrow and despair. The courageous ones are the ones who face fear and accept failure and still keep going, even in the most difficult of circumstances. In the darkest of dark nights, the source of our courage will help us discover the symbolic light and the laughter and the joyfulness of life.

The gift of courage, to ourselves and to others, is the gift of love. The most courageous feat that we may do is to embrace the divine love of the earth and the unseen world. We have to be fearless, without doubt, and live in a manner where all actions and reactions are courageous and a reflection of this pristine love. It takes courage to let go of our past by righting the wrongs of the past and doing right action in the present. This results in a life of wonderment and happiness. But only we have the freedom to do this. No one else will do it for us.

Courage strengthens us to take risks in life and to persevere in the face of difficulties that would stop others. As a compassionate earth warrior, have the courage to embrace life to its fullest and express kindhearted attitudes to all, no matter whether the person is a friend or a foe. Embrace the courage and strength of Þórr—and his overwhelming fearlessness.

⚜

A fearless mind and spirit is not the absence or suppression of fear. Only a fool's ego or drug/alcohol-induced bravado would shout "I am fearless" in certain life-and-death situations. Fear is sometimes necessary. Without fear, there would be a flat line of emotion in the presence of the unknown. The Vikings were superior warriors. They understood fear, the detachment to it and the "pressing-down" of it. Pressing-down refers to the process of the acknowledgement of fear during conflict but it is pressed down only to be purged later on after battle or conflict. This is not the suppression or denial of fear where fear stays hidden but is still active within a person's behaviors, patterns of being and actions. This is the fear during conflict, which is still there, but it does not affect our minds or our actions. After the battle is finished, it is then purged.

⚜

Fearlessness comes down to two things: the amount of fear and the attachment to it. The less there is of the unknown—by us having more experiences of life—the less we fear, although fear is still present. In life, there is a necessity for a bit of fear. It lets us feel alive. Driving all alone in the dark to the stream to bathe takes me close to an hour. Even after years of this type of practice, there are still always a few grains of fear on my drive to the stream. Once there, the fear is shed in the same way that I drop my clothes to enter the stream. I detach from any apprehension or fear of the excessive cold, the ice-covered, swiftly flowing waters, or the dark.

Fearlessness, a total regeneration of our being, comes from detachment—pure and simple. Detachment is the key element not only in achieving a fearless spirit but, in addition, attaining great spiritual and healing power. Fearlessness may then be looked at as achieving a state of mental tranquility. Our mind is not attached. It is not chattering with issues of the past, present, and/or future that upset our mental state of peace and harmony. This state of detachment and mental tranquility results in a strong and powerful mind.

Strong Mind, Strong Intention, Strong Will

Norse warriors were feared due to their unbridled and furious fighting spirit in the shield wall. It was a reflection of their strong mind where kinship, honor, and detachment to death were foremost in their consciousness. They were homesteaders only part of the year. When not farming, they voyaged into the unknown, seeking knowledge and new lands. This took a fearless and resolute heart and a strong mind.

A strong mind is a nondualistic mind. An "ordinary" mind is a dualistic mind, ever seeking safety and security and viewing all reality through the prism of right and wrong, success and failure, past and future. This dualistic mind generates tension and stress in the body. If you have a strong mind, you live in the present, only visiting the past and future under your own choice and power, and there is no concept of success or failure, and therefore, no body tension and thus less of an opportunity for disharmony and dis-ease to occur within the body. When we are in the present with full sensory awareness, we are engaging the total power of our mind.

When we have a strong mind, our intentions are strong and so is our will. These result in right thought and right action. Þórr hurls his hammer with such a strong intent and will that it never misses and always returns to him. In other words, whatever and wherever we focus our attention with a strong will and intention will manifest, if it's part of the sisters weaving, and for good or ill, the intent will return to us. For every action, there is a reaction. There are consequences to our actions, and we must be responsible for those actions. Not accepting responsibility is a sign of a weak mind.

Right action is not as straightforward as it seems to be. One of the Buddhist Precepts is right action. Precepts are not commandments but how we live and respond to life's struggles. Another precept is not killing. This leads us to the assumption that a right action is not killing. The reality is that in our life struggles right action is circumstantial. Right action depends on circumstances. In certain circumstances not killing would be a right action but, and a big but, in other circumstances such as when our loved ones are in danger of being killed, the right action would be killing the antagonist. One person's terrorist is another person's freedom fighter. In other words, there are no absolutes; true right action flows from our awakened hearts and strong minds.

Þórr and Giants

A blinding snowstorm with excessive cold could spell death for anyone caught out in it—due to the wrath of a frost giant. Very possibly the origination of giants came from the observation of natural phenomena, according to Rudolf Simek. He states that "Giants are natural spirits and among the original inhabitants of the world. In Germanic cosmogony, the world is created from a giant, Ymir, and the daughters of a race of primeval giants give birth to the first

Nordic gods. Odin, Vili, and Vé, for instance, come from the giantess Bestla."[135] According to Jón Hnefill Aðalsteinsson, the "similarity between gods and the giants implies a godlike quality to the giants, who nonetheless retain their close links with nature."[136] Since there is "no clear distinction between the gods and the giants,"[137] what better way to subconsciously push your one-god Christian agenda than demonizing the giants? Thus, we must be careful and discerning when turning to the *Prose Edda* for knowledge.

One of the roles of Þórr was as defender of gods and humans against hostile elemental and threatening forces such as the giants and the Midgard serpent. We must remember though, all forces of nature may be destructive (chaotic) but also constructive (ordered).

Mjǫllnir

Ever since the first humans gazed up at a tumultuous night sky with thunder rumbling in the distance, the darkness separated by spears of light, people have been in awe and frightened of these heavenly wonders and powers. The booming thunder was the drums of the gods calling forth the fire of heaven and the tears of the goddess—tears that would fertilize the earth into a fruitful paradise. Out of terror came beauty, fruitfulness, and life. It is only reasonable that the god who represented this power would be awe-inspiring and powerful. This is Þórr, Son of Life's Struggles, wielding Mjǫllnir for the benefit of the earth and humanity.

Forged by cunning dwarves with a unique short handle, Mjǫllnir symbolizes sanctification, holiness, lightning, and enlightenment. Sanctification is the process to make sacred, holy, or pure; to set apart for sacred use; to consecrate; to bless. Besides blessing, Mjǫllnir has the power to smash through the limitations of a closed and clouded mind. Moreover, Mjǫllnir, as thunderbolt, is symbolic of protection, creativity, and fertility.

Þórr wears *megingjǫrð*, a strength-giving belt, and two iron gloves. This belt of power is *megin* (strength) and *jǫrð* (earth). In other words, *megingjǫrð* is the strength of the earth, or gravity. The gloves represent the dualistic polarities—positive and negative. With the assistance of these gloves, Þórr is able to throw Mjǫllnir. When he grabs Mjǫllnir with both hands to hurl it, a secret is revealed to us. The blending of the dualities, positive and negative, provides not only light[138] (lightning) but divine will and powerful intention.

When thrown, it always returns to his hand. This is the indomitable power of thought over matter (see the tale of the Brawler in the next section). And most importantly, the thoughts we put out do return to us—ponder this as to your life.

⚜

Double-headed Mjǫllnir is representative of ancient double-headed stone axes or hammers, which are primordial symbols, possibly of Hyperborean origin. Both of these symbolic weapons represent the lightning bolt. When thunder and lightning crashed across the sky, it was believed that thunderstones and lightning stones fell to the earth. Many of these stones were meteorites. "Many ancient peoples attributed meteorites to the same god as the one that caused lightning and thunder. Meteorites, lightning-struck stones, and prehistoric stone axes found in the earth were all thought to be objects hurled from heaven when thunder crashed.

Iron meteorites provided iron for people to use for tools and weapons before the art of smelting was known. Finding such meteorites was rare and the ancients did understand the meteorites' connection with sky. This was evidenced in the names given to them. The ancient Egyptians called meteorites the "stones of heaven." The oldest Sumerian word for iron meant "sky" and "fire." The Hittites, one of the first to use weapons from smelted terrestrial iron, called the metal "fire from heaven."[139]

Another symbolic thunderstone and lightning stone was flint, as it has the power to create fire. For this reason, it was mystically connected to thunder and lightning. The Norse were not alone in this belief. In the inner teachings of the Hebrew Torah, the divine spark within us is compared to the "fire in the flint." It lies dormant until awoken. Even submerged in water, the "fire in the flint" is never extinguished, just as our immortal spark is never destroyed. It is always there as a potential force. This illustrates the power of Mjǫllnir as best demonstrated by the tale of the brawler.

Hrungnir

The mightiest of all the giants was Hrungnir, Old Norse for "the Brawler." When he got drunk, he became angry and belligerent. This eventually led to his downfall. The following is an abbreviated telling of the myth of the duel between Þórr and Hrungnir.

According to the tale, while Þórr was in the east fighting trolls, Óðinn entered Jǫtunheimar, world of the giants, and made a wager with Hrungnir as to who had the finer horse. This resulted in a horse race—Óðinn on his eight-legged steed Sleipnir and Hrungnir on his horse Gullfaxi (gold mane). But of course, Óðinn was uncatchable, and before Hrungnir knew it, blinded by his own need to win, he had inadvertently entered Asgard. But after such a contest as this, the Aesir decided to share ale and mead with Hrungnir as befitting any visiting guest, even though he had not been invited. Due to the giant's nature, Hrungnir drank too much and became belligerent and boastful, bragging he would crush Asgard into the sea and take Valhǫll with him back to Jǫtunheimar along with Freyja and Sif. It was at this point that Þórr arrived on the scene, angry and ready to slay the unarmed giant. In turn, Hrungnir accused Þórr of being a coward to slay an unarmed opponent and challenged him to a duel. Of course, Þórr readily accepted.

The dueling field was on the outskirts of Jǫtunheimar. Hrungnir, with a heart and head of stone, walked onto the field of battle clad in stone armor with a stone shield and his chosen weapon—a whetstone. With a clap of thunder and a bolt of lightning, Þórr, eyes blazing, roared onto the battlefield. Without hesitation, Þórr hurled Mjǫllnir toward Hrungnir's head. In response, the giant threw his whetstone. They met in midair, where the whetstone shattered but Mjǫllnir continued on, hitting its mark and crushing Hrungnir's skull, killing him. Pieces of the whetstone fell to earth, but one lodged in Þórr's forehead.

What hidden meanings and teachings are embedded within this tale? Þórr's directed thought and strong mind broke the whetstone. In other words, a strong mind and directed thought can penetrate matter to destroy or create and, in the process, restore harmony.

Could another teaching be the triumph of will over desire? In some ways, Hrungnir reflects first-chakra issues (please see the next chapter). One of the first chakra issues is procreation. This is symbolized by Hrungnir's desire for the goddesses. The stone shield reveals a mind that is unawakened and dualistic, and a heart of stone comes from greed and unresolved issues and the various woundings of life. A stone heart leads to cruelty with a lack of empathy or sympathy for others.

Þórr's directed action and will shatters these aspects of Hrungnir. This leads to Þórr's enlightenment, so to speak, through the embedded whetstone (fire contained within stone) in his forehead. Of course, we will never be able to discern if these were the actual hidden teachings in the original telling of this tale. But taking these teachings to heart will make us better individuals with increased frith, honor, and luck.

Luck

The majority of people believe that luck is nothing more than chance. If you're a Christian, not only do you believe in chance but also grace, which is "a Christian theological term denoting divine gifts without which human salvation would be impossible."[140] Both of these beliefs are external to us and out of our control. They are not dependent on our hearts, our minds, or our spirits. With these beliefs, there is no need to strengthen our mind and spirit or awaken our heart.

These beliefs are not Norse-Germanic. Being lucky or unlucky is not chance but a reflection of us, a reflection of our minds. Accordingly, "the inner state of a man in luck is described in Icelandic as a whole mind, *heill hugr*, which of course comprises wisdom as well as goodwill and affection. The man of whole mind is true to his kin and his friends, stern to his enemies, and easy to get on with, when lesser men come seeking aid. His redes are really good gifts to the receiver—whole redes, in Icelandic *heil ráð*."[141]

The ancient word *rede* means "counsel, advice." It goes hand in hand with luck. It "is a perfect illustration of Teutonic psychology. When given to others, it means counsel; when applied to the luck working within the mind, it means wisdom, or a good plan, and from an ethical point of view, just and honest thoughts. But the word naturally includes the idea of success, which accompanies wise and upright devising, and on the other hand power and authority, which are the working of a sound will."[142] Likewise, "a redeless man is weakened by lack of will, lack of power, and lack of self-assertion."[143]

Words and actions reflect a person's luck. A person who continuously lies or tells half-truths would be known to have unluck and recognized as a *níðing*. This person lacks honor and courage with the connotation of being a villain.

Luck, then, is the power that inspires a man and emanates from his person, filling his words and his deeds; it comprises all the requirements of the family, its powers and possibilities, its accomplishments and its hope, its genius and character. Luck contains the very existence of the clan; the family is called *kynsæll*, lucky in kinship, when kinsmen are numerous and new members are constantly being born to fill the places falling vacant.[144]

It makes sense then that a strong and powerful mind and a strong will—in other words, luck—are under Þórr's guidance as protector of humanity and the earth. Once again, we see how the attributes of Þórr may guide us and assist us in overcoming our struggles of life. A mind that is powerful and resolute with total focus, intent, and will, without any extraneous chattering or mind-talk is developed through the practice of becoming one with nature. This ability is cultivated through participation mystique. This is a knowing of the things of life and their inherent mysteries through the experience of the mundane as well as the spiritual. Participation mystique may be as simple as sitting alone under a tree and listening to the sounds of nature and our own hearts, or as complex as dawn bathing in a stream. Additional practices and actions may include such things as fasting and exposure to the elements. When I lived on the coast of Maine, every time there was a Nor'easter, I ran to the edge of the ocean cliffs and experienced through all my senses, absorbed through my whole body, the power of the storm—one with the essence and force of Þórr's power. Participation mystique is essential and will result in a transformation of consciousness—and magic happens. When we are one with nature, we may elicit acts that others may view as miraculous, such as calming or calling the wind.

However, the present-day technology of smartphones and social media is a hindrance to a strong mind and these abilities. If need be, it would be best to use both sparingly. A strong mind is a mind of luck—a Norse mind, where there is no separation between the soul and the body. This is just not human bodies but all bodies—stones, trees, animals, and so forth. In other words, a strong mind is a consciousness of unity or radical nonduality.

Hamingja

It can be very confusing when we discuss the various spiritual expressions of our soul. We have explored the concept of *fylgja*—a guardian spirit. Next, we discussed *hamr*—our birth guardian. Finally, we arrive at the concept of *hamingja*—loosely identifiable as an ancestral guardian. Classifying it as an ancestral guardian doesn't reveal to us the totality of its meaning and essence. Hamingja is connected with luck—in other words, soul.

Hamingja is best classified as ancestral power—divine power based on our soul. This inner power may be seen with the eyes and contained with the hands. "The king's hamingja passes like a warmth from his hand into the warrior whose hand he grasps; his hamingja enters as a force into men and fills their bodies, penetrating to the outermost joints, and from these over into their weapons."[145] As was stated in chapter 1, "One can recognise a hero of the past in one's contemporary, by his courage, and by the contents and strength of his honour, but also his career provides its evidence, and this perhaps of the clearest, as to the connection between past and present."[146] This would be the hero's hamingja—our intrinsic, ancestral, inborn power. This power is consistent with one's inner nature. It can be sought, but seeking does not guarantee that one will attain it.

Loki: Who or What is Loki?

In closing this chapter on Þórr, let's delve into the enigmatic nature of Loki. Within the mythic structure of the Norse, there seems to be a lack of clarity surrounding the character named Loki. What or who is Loki? Enigmatic as he is, *what* is a better word than *who*. Loki is the father of all that seemingly is (using a Christian term) "evil": Hel, the wolf Fenrir (greed and gluttony), and the world serpent Jörmungandr (separation of known from unknown). Many times throughout the myths, Loki is joined at the hip with Þórr and often interacts with Óðinn. There is further mystery in determining if he is a god or jǫtunn —or his he possibly both? Additionally, there is the question of Loki's function during the end times of Ragnarok—assisting the giants against the gods.

So does Loki embody all that is dualistically "bad" in opposition to all the "good" of the Norse myths and life? Supposedly he caused the death of the pure god of light Baldur. This would be recognized as an act of pure evil. For this act, he was chained to a rock (three, in fact). Sound familiar? Loki also has a dual nature, causing chaos but then restoring order out of the chaos of his own making. Keep this in mind.

Furthermore, he is definitely portrayed as a trickster, a deceiver, a shape changer, and maker of mischief. Is Loki a shamanic figure? He did shape change and display transvestite behaviors—a trait of shamanism—but so did Óðinn and Þórr. Finally, the burning star Sirius was called "Lokabrenna" by the Norse, which meant "Loki's torch" or "burning by Loki."

⚜

Is fire evil? If your house is burning down, you would possibly answer yes. If you are lost in the woods and fire is the only way to stay warm and survive, you would most definitely answer no. Forest fires are seemingly destructive and may be deadly. The only way to stop the fires gluttony is to deprive it of its food source. Are these fires evil? No, it is nature's way of rejuvenation and rebirth of the ecosystem.

Fire embodies polarity—chaos and order. It creates and destroys. As we all know, "fire consumes, warms, and illuminates, but can also bring pain and death; thus, its symbolic meaning varies wildly, depending upon the context of its use. It is often the symbol of inspiration, and yet it is also the predominant symbol of Hell."[147] It is the only element "that humans can produce themselves, so it bridges the connection between the mortals and gods. Rituals often involve an eternal flame, and kindling a fire is equated with birth and resurrection."[148]

And then we have the concept of "need-fire," which is fire resulting from the friction between two inert materials. It is a central principle of the rune *Nauðiz*. Furthermore, necessity is one of the defining meanings of Nauðiz. Our internal stress may be transformed into strength and power through the mysterious need-fire. We may either surrender to our stress or transform it; this is the realm of Nauðiz. Part of the transformation occurs through a change in thinking and an alteration in our external situations causing the stress.

Fire is the purification element of the heavens while water is the earth's purifier. Our spiritual goal is the reconciliation of these two opposing elements, or the blending of them where we are able to wash with fire and to burn with water. Fire symbolizes spirit, *spirit* meaning not only the unseen or otherworld but one's aspect of self: body, mind, emotion, and spirit. And just as fire may bring life or death, we may have an altruistic spirit or a greedy one.

Where do all these facts lead us? To Loki's possible identity, which is the power and force of fire (such as a lightning-struck tree). According to Randi Barndon, "In Norse mythology Loki was the master of fire similar to Prometheus."[149] However, Loki is not to be taken as a deity of fire per se but the essence and embodiment of fire in its metaphysical and physical attributes (such as the hearth fire).

The Longhouse, the Hearth Fire, and the Lightning-Struck Tree

> Is it true; is it not
> That the little ones
> Lack the spirit?
> Is it not a lack of light?
> How can these be in dark?
> It is time: Summon the Serpents
> Those of Light: It is time
> It is part of the whole of life
> Let us rejoice in their light.

My wife and I are fortunate enough to have been in a British Columbia longhouse during the Northwest Coast First People's winter dance season. Even though the indigenous people no longer live in these longhouses, they are still used in their spiritual practices. We were with our teachers, Vince and Mom Stogan. Much of what we experienced can't be written down or told except for the ceremonial setting. The spirit dances are held at night. The only warmth and light is provided by a large, open fire in the middle of the longhouse. The open fire provides not only the physical comfort of heat and light but is also the metaphysical symbol of spirit.

The northern cultures of the Americas were not the only ones to live in longhouses. Various other ancient cultures in northern climes, such as the

Norse, also called longhouses home. In the middle of these longhouses were hearths with its central fire—the essence of life. The hearth fire was the soul of the home and the core to survival and sanity during the long, stormy winter nights and days.

During the fifties, a stone was discovered on a Danish beach—the Snaptun Stone. An image of Loki is carved on the stone. This Viking Age stone is not only decorative but was a functioning hearthstone as well. At the bottom of the stone, beneath the depiction of Loki, "there is a hole, through which a bellows would be placed and used to stoke the hearth fire. The hearthstone not only protected people from the intensity of the flames, but also acted as a shield protecting the bellows from catching fire as well."[150]

Besides this hearthstone, "there are other folk customs that connect Loki with the hearth fire. In Norway there's a custom of feeding leftovers into the hearth/kitchen fire. In Norwegian folk belief, just as thunder is associated with Thor, the crackling in the hearth fire is associated with Loki."[151] The rune for the hearth fire is *Kenaz*—Loki's rune. It is the focused, controlled fire of the hearth. Kenaz (torch) symbolizes the divine spark within, creativity, and the fiery spark within us that transforms and creates. It is the transition from one state to another. Just as the divine spark within us is hidden, so too is the complex identity of Loki buried deep within the legends and myths. This has led to much misinformation concerning who or what he is.

Throughout the Norse legends, Loki and Þórr share many adventures together. As I said before, it seems they are joined at the hip. And they are. Þórr is thunder. And what many times accompanies thunder is lightning. As an essence of fire, Loki symbolizes the potential of fire from lightning, i.e., a lightning-struck tree. Lightning-struck trees are sacred, a blending of the fire of heaven with the wood of the earth. As my wife and I learned from Vince Stogan, placing a piece of burnt wood from a lightning-struck tree above the entrance to a home will protect it from fire.

"Lightning and fire are so closely related to life and procreation that modern scientists believe that the first physical creation of life on Earth took place when a bolt of lightning struck the primeval chemical 'soup' which covered the face of our earth at that time—thus, literally, becoming the first 'spark of life.'"[152] This would be a microcosmic happening reflecting the macrocosmic event when the unknown absolute reflected itself, creating a "spark of divine life" within all things of the seen and unseen universe.

"Fire, brought to man from the heavens by a bolt of lightning, and humanity's courage in taming the flame made an indelible impression upon our prehistoric ancestors. This is the essence of the oldest myths, the almost universal story of the Tree of Fire and Knowledge, a.k.a. the Tree of Life, the Burning Tree, the Burning Bush, etc."[153]

Óðinn's Wisdom
Power of Spirit

CHAPTER 7

Óðinn

I know that I hung in the windtorn tree
Nine whole nights, spear-pierced,
Consecrated to Óðinn, myself to my Self above me in the tree,
Whose root no one knows whence it sprang.

None brought me bread, none served me drink;
I searched the depths, spied runes of wisdom;
Raised them with song, and fell once more thence.
—HÁVAMÁL[154]

Óðinn is the Germanic (Wotan) and Norse god of wisdom and the magical arts of speech—poetry and chant - galdr. Óðinn has many dimensions to his essence. He is an enigmatic wanderer, ever seeking knowledge and wisdom. He is wise, ingenious, and all-powerful. But on the other hand, he is a thief, a warmonger, and he is wild, restless, and vehement.

Even though Óðinn is an enigma, his primary aspect is as Allfather, which may have originated from a primordial, all-encompassing deity. As Allfather, Óðinn's hypostases, his essential nature, is threefold. This took the form of Óðinn himself and his two companions: Lóðurr and Hœnir. Óðinn represented the gift of breath—spirit/soul; Lóðurr the gifts of movement and physical things—body; Hœnir the gift of consciousness—mind. In other words, "as Allfather, he is the divine root of every being in all the worlds, the essence of divinity present in all life forms, in the smallest particle as well as in the cosmos itself."[155] Thus Óðinn would represent the concept of the reflective absolute that interpenetrates the relativeness of the universe.

Óðinn is an archetype of the primordial knowledge of the interpenetrative radical nonduality of all things such as the nonduality of wisdom and stupidity. One key to this knowledge is to be discovered in his numerous names—over two hundred. He is known as the "truth finder" as well as the "harm worker," "deceiver," and "nourisher." He is cunning and deceitful but also truth seeking and benevolent.

Another clue to his universality is revealed in his possession of a magic ring, "which dispenses eight more like itself every ninth night. This evidently refers to proliferating cycles wherein each curl, comprising a number of smaller curls, represents recurrent motion in both time and space: the wheels within wheels of biblical symbology. This spiral design can be found among plants and animals throughout nature, from the atomic worlds to the great sweeping movements of stars and galaxies in space."[156]

In another guise, Óðinn's gift of breath identifies him as a wind god and a god of inspiration. He is a seeker of knowledge and wisdom. Óðinn, as the wandering truth seeker and walker between worlds, is recognizable as a shaman. He possesses the attributes that identify a person as a shaman, such as being a shape shifter, psychopomp, and having four guardians spirits—two wolves and two ravens. Additionally, Sleipnir, Óðinn's eight-legged steed, illustrates his means of travel throughout the universe (both the seen and unseen worlds). One of the motifs of the shaman is his or her journeying to the heavens or the underworld by means of riding on a bird or an animal. The uniqueness of Sleipnir is his eight legs, which may symbolize the four major and four minor directions. Eight also equates to infinity. With horse and rider plus eight legs, we have not only the eight directions but up (heavens) and down (underworld), a total of ten—a divine number symbolizing the divine manifest universe. Does this symbolize the eternalness of Óðinn, even though he is supposed to die at Ragnarok? What do you think?

As a person of power, Óðinn can also be considered a wizard, sorcerer (as one who influences fate), and a battle god. But what stands out more than any of these labels is his willingness to sacrifice self for knowledge and wisdom. It makes sense in our quest to awaken—Óðinn's essential sacrifice may be an example and guide for us to follow.

Sacrifice

If you read Hávamál, *it's about how to meet other cultures and be a good guest or host to the world around you. These are ancient sayings for the traveler—not for the guy sitting at home on his ass thinking his living room is the centre of the world.*
—HILMAR ÖRN HILMARSSON

A prime action of accumulating knowledge, power, and wisdom is to be found within the concept of sacrifice. To acquire power, we need to sacrifice the accepted materialistic norms of society. In other words, a person totally immersed in a materialistic culture has no time for spiritual pursuits; it's all about money. This type of person is unwilling to sacrifice their time for any pursuits other than the one that will bring them more materialistic status and wealth. Óðinn was not as the above quote states, "sitting at home on his ass thinking his living room is the centre of the world." He was a wanderer continually seeking knowledge and wisdom. For us to be a wanderer of foreign, unknown lands, we need to sacrifice time and money. If you follow a Norse-Germanic tradition and have never set foot in those lands, you only have a hollow mental understanding of these traditions.

I teach an old-school Japanese martial art. My first of many journeys to Japan was in 1983. I now have an understanding of the land, the people, and most importantly, the landvættir. It is the same with spiritual traditions from climbing the Tor in 1981, to walking the Inca Trail to Machu Picchu in 1988, to being clawed by a jaguar shape changer in an underground temple deep in the Yucatan Jungles in 1990, to the hidden ones in Iceland in 2012. These are just a few of my many worldwide experiences. All of these journeys required great sacrifice—emotionally and financially. In fact, our first journey to England, Wales, and Scotland came at the expense of not having a new roof on our home. We choose the journey over the roof. How about you? Are you willing to sacrifice time and money to journey into the unknown?

⚜

Blót was and still is one of the traditional forms of sacrifice. "The word *blót* (Icelandic and Faroese: *blót*) is the Old Norse and Old English representative of the Proto-Germanic noun *blōtq* 'sacrifice, worship.'"[157] This was "men's active relation to the gods, contains the full potency of the religious act. It expresses man's power to transform an object of ordinary holiness so that it becomes filled with the power of divinity and passes on strength into the human world. When Floki was about to set out for Iceland, he held a great sacrifice and blot-ed three ravens, which were to show him the way. Then he built a cairn on the spot where the blot had taken place, and put to sea:"[158]

> The worshipper went to his grove and to his gods in search of strength, and he would not have to go in vain; but it was no use his constantly presenting himself as receptive, and quietly waiting to be filled with all good gifts. It was his business to make the gods human, in the old, profound sense of the word, where the emphasis lies on an identification and consequent conjunction of soul with soul. Without mingling mind, there was no possibility of union here in Middle-garth, he who could not inspire his neighbor with himself never became his friend, and no will could reach from the one to the other. The gods themselves could do nothing then, nay willed nothing before those who invoked them had rendered them living, as Floki bloted the ravens. It was men who rendered the gods gracious, not by awakening their sympathy, but by inspiring them with frith of their frith...
>
> With regard to the ceremonial acts which brought about the fusion of the human and divine, we have but scanty information. Gods and men no doubt shared their meat offering; the greater part of the sacrificial meat found its way to the table at the feast, and a portion, we may suppose, went to the blot house.[159]

I believe that another means of ritualistically and ceremonially[160] uniting the divine and human was through Óðinn's practice of sacrifice self to self.

Sacrifice Self to Self
Óðinn's primary sacrifices were known as self to self: (*gefinn Óðni*) myself to myself. What does this mean? Is it the same as self-sacrifice? Not quite. Sacrifice

self to self is slightly different. Self-sacrifice means some type of personal sacrifice for the benefit of others. This could take the form of a single parent working two jobs or a person rushing into a burning building to save others. However, sacrifice that is self to self has slightly different connotations. It is still self-sacrifice but with the caveat that we must first know ourselves to be able to sacrifice our self to self. This is self-sacrifice in the pursuit of understanding and knowledge about ourselves that we will use to help others grow and evolve. It is a sacrifice for the greater well-being of humanity and the earth.

A sacrifice of self to self is usually one that others are unwilling to make such as Óðinn's sacrifice of one of his eyes for wisdom—to drink daily of the well of knowledge, Mimir's well. What is important to note here is that Mimir's well symbolizes matter. Only by our immersion in the world of matter (nature), where both love and fear reside, are we able to achieve the experiences that provide us with knowledge and wisdom.

Since Óðinn's sacrifice was one of his eyes, this reveals to us the truth that we must sacrifice our own illusions and egocentric, dualistic selves for our true selves: our divine human self. But as I have noted, this was not Óðinn's only sacrifice. He also sacrificed by hanging on the world tree, Yggdrasill, for nine nights, and through his sufferings, he received the knowledge of the runes and brought the power of speech to humanity.

It is important to note that it is not necessary to hang from a tree for nine nights to sacrifice self to self. The sacrifice is real, but the story is mythological. There is another form of sacrificing self to self that has been practiced for thousands of years. This is consciously drowning or what is known as bathing-ritual submersion in water, an experience of death in life. As a sacrifice of self to self, bathing is done in the winter; fasting is necessary and sleep is sacrificed as we must bathe right before first light; we must journey to a swiftly flowing stream preferably in the mountains and then we must sacrifice our self-concern as we submerge three to four times in the cold, dark waters. There are many forms of sacrificing self to self. One would be a fast of food and sleep. Another would be a solitary quest wandering through the mountains and valleys with a minimum of food and water. A third would be galdr while standing under a waterfall. Is it time for you to begin sacrificing self to self if you have not already?

Blót—Burnings

The most common blót takes the form of veneration to the gods and goddesses and ancestors through the sharing of ale, drinking toasts, with them, such as the ceremony of the Ale horn:

> Among the Northmen, the usual term for the blot-cup seems to have been *full*, a word whose old-fashioned structure speaks of age and dignity, and the meaning of which serves equally well to cover fullness, the state of being filled, or abundance, and that which is full. Another sacred word is *veig*, which, whatever may have been its original meaning, comprises the thought of strength and honour...
>
> The effect of emptying the cup was first and foremost a community of feeling—for harvest and peace runs the wish of blessing. Men drank together and drank themselves together, as the old saying goes, in the ancestral brew of power. The assembly was made one, and this unifying force of the drink is expressed in the ceremonial which requires that the horn shall pass from man to man round the hall; the chain must be unbroken, and close upon itself again—the assembly should be made one.[161]

Next, we have the more extensive blót consisting of animal sacrifice. As we all know, the destructive incursion of Christianity into Norse-Germanic lands decimated indigenous religious beliefs and practices. Even though this was the case, their practices and ceremonies continued, shall we say, underground for unknown generations. Eventually, any trace of the ceremonies such as blót and the oral transmission of conducting it were lost to the passage of time. To reconstruct these ceremonies is very difficult. Where then can we turn in our attempt to understand and possibly reconstruct these ceremonies?

Outside of possibly unreliable written sources and the findings of archeology, the key to our discovery of this lost knowledge is found within indigenous cultures that still practice and conduct ceremonies that have been orally handed down, generation after generation. We would need to discover ceremonies that would parallel Norse-Germanic ones such as blót. One such ceremony is called "feeding the spirits." Spirits include the ancestors, the spirits of the land, and the forgotten ones. In this context, it is important to note that the blót "recipients of sacrifice are as varied as the goals of sacrifice. Sacrifices were given to spiritual beings such as the heathen gods (*goð*); elves (*álfar*); female guardian spirits (*dísir*) and other spirits (*vœttir*); dead ancestors; animals (who were often representative of particular gods—for example, ravens for Óðin, goats for Þórr, horses or boars for Freyr, and so on); and even to groves or waterfalls. This provides a context in which *blóta* extends its meaning from 'sacrifice' to 'worship,' since the act of making a sacrifice to these recipients is also understood as identical to worship."[162] Even though the term *worship* is used, I prefer to acknowledge it as honoring the otherworld, not a worship of it.

Ancestor veneration is a foundational worldview of indigenous people. It is also deeply ingrained into the Norse-Germanic mind, as is the belief and veneration of the spirits of the land, hidden ones (elves, faeries, and so forth) and the ancestors. The primary honoring of these spirits and the gods takes the form of veneration through the ceremonial blót.

The importance of our ancestors is reflected in our hamingja. "The hamingja as it reveals itself in its human representatives is concentrated in the ancestor, who was present in the blót, acting the deeds of the past through his friends. He is god and he is not god, according to our nomenclature. Like the ring and other treasures which are at the same time earthly life wedging into the invisible and the invisible thrusting into the everyday, the ancestor may be regarded as the divine reaching into man or man extending into the divine."[163] Taking into account the preceding and the importance of kin and kinship to the Norse-Germanic people, we must consider that a blót may honor the divine (gods), but most importantly is the veneration of the ancestors and the hidden ones (spirits).

When we discuss the divine, we must keep in mind the concept of radical nonduality—the divine within us and us in the divine:

> Between man and god there exists no difference of kind, but there is a vital distinction of degree, the gods being the whole hamingja, whereas men are only part. The boundary between gods and men is permanent, but varying in place; it is shifted downward when men go about on their daily round of business, and it may be pushed upward when they assume their garment of holiness and sally out in a body to fight or to fish. Only in the blot is the boundary line obliterated, but then during feast time there are no men, because the hamingja is all and in all. The divineness of men when in a state of holiness is revealed

by the metaphors of poetry; when the warrior is called the god of the sword or the god of battle, the expression is nothing but matter-of-fact description. The same reality appears in the naming of woman as the goddess of trinkets, and still more significantly as the ale goddess, referring to her holy office in the drink offering.[164]

Location of a blót is important. But there are varying views on which location, in nature or in a *hof* (temple) or in a separate *blóthof* ("sacrificial, heathen temple"). Since few of us will be building a special temple for sacrifices, the best location for a blót is in nature. Most importantly, you want no human-made separation between us and the unseen powers of the earth and heaven. And conducting a blót barefoot allows us to have a direct connection from our body to the body of the earth. Being in nature and barefoot is how I conduct the ceremony of "feeding the spirits." Evidence of ceremonial feeding of the dead, spirits of the land, and ancestors can be traced all the way back to the ancient Egyptians and is alluded to in the story of "The Twelfth Labor of Heracles." While Heracles was in the Underworld, seeking to capture the furious three-headed dog with a mane of snakes known as the Cerberus, he decided to give thanks to the dead by sacrificing one of Hades's (the lord of the Underworld's) cattle. It is interesting to note that "functionally speaking, Thor is related to the mythical Herakles/Hercules of the ancient world."[165]

⚜

Feeding the spirits of the dead is most difficult and dangerous, and could be considered the supreme compassionate, ceremonial, indigenous religious practice. Nonetheless, there is still one dark blemish on this premier spiritual practice: down through history and throughout various cultures, there have been times when humans, even children, have become the sacrificial food of the gods.

Feeding the spirits or doing a burning is one of the shamanic/religious practices and power handed down to my wife and I by the late shamans Mom and Vince Stogan. Since this knowledge was and still is orally transmitted, I can only reveal a few things that are similar to a blót. Before we open the ceremony by calling in the spirits, I paint myself and my wife with red paint, symbolic of blood. Three plates of food are always required: for the ancient ones, the spirits of the land, and most importantly, the forgotten ones.

In the early nineties, we conducted a burning on the Big Island of Hawaii. My Hawaiian healer friend was pleased and expressed disbelief that we would be willing to conduct a ceremony honoring their ancestors. He was equally amazed that we had the knowledge and power to do this spiritual work. Ages ago, his people had conducted this ceremony but the knowledge of the ceremony had been lost.

We conducted the burning late on a Saturday afternoon. The next morning at the White Sand Beach, my friend gave me a message from one of his ancestors who came to him during the burning. "My ancestor brought me a message, but it's for you. My ancestor said that you are a *kahuna po'o* (high priest)...you are a prophet bringing back 'first knowledge'—the lost knowledge and sacred teachings that have been misunderstood, forgotten, and corrupted."

⚜

Conducting a burning is very stressful to say the least. There are many tales to be told of burnings, which fly in the face of accepted scientific fact. One such example comes from my own experience:

We were conducting a memorial burning for my father who had passed over the year before. The plate of food for my father would include foods that he liked and would have eaten while he was alive. After calling in the spirits, the plates of food are then put on the "table" as an offering. As Sherry handed me my father's plate, I saw that it contained a piece of wheat bread—something that my father did not like and would not eat. The brief thought that flowed through my mind was: *Wheat bread—Dad hates this...*

Once I finished laying the rest of the plates, cups, and other things on the table, I lit the fire. Time passed as we each conversed silently with our loved ones who had passed over. During this time, we each observed the impossible. The wheat bread did not burn while everything else around it, all the other food, burned to ashes. The wheat bread was untouched.

After I closed the ceremony, I turned to Sherry and said, "How come wheat bread? You know my father hated it."

"I know," she replied, "but your mother said she hasn't had white bread in the house since your father died." Sherry paused and smiled. "She said that it was the only bread she had and he would have to eat it!"

Týr's Sacrifice—the Beast

I would expect that many people are aware of the saying "beware of a wolf in sheep's clothing." Who has not heard of Little Red Riding Hood. Navaho call shamans that practice black magic "wolf." In some instances, European mythology negatively refers to "the relationship between wolves and men in the use of the word 'wolf' or 'wolf's head' for an outlaw, and the legend of the werewolf, a skin changer who turns into a wolf when the moon is full...Perhaps it is the very similarities between wolves and humans that contribute to the terror they inspire in European legend. We fear the wolf outside because we are too aware of the power of the wolf within."[166] Add to this the Norse-Germanic legend of a gigantic wolf named Fenrir and fierce warriors—berserkers—and we can see why the Northern European people considered the ferocious and cunning wolf the metaphoric beast within.

Fenrir, also known as *Fenrisúlfr* (Fenris wolf), was birthed by Loki. The wolf had two younger siblings: his sister, Hel, and his brother, the serpent, Jormungand, also known as the Midgard Serpent. As a pup, only the god Týr had the courage to approach Fenrir. After the wolf's birth, there were prophecies that at the end of time, at the battle of Ragnarok, Fenrir would swallow and kill the Allfather. The quandary facing the Norse gods and goddess was that they couldn't kill Fenrir, as that would defile and desecrate Asgard—their homeland. Since killing was out of the question, they still needed some way to control his violent impulses. As he was growing larger day-by-day, they needed to bind the beast and control its violent instincts and compulsions. Twice they attempted to chain him but failed.

To bind Fenrir, Týr—god of honor and justice—made a self-sacrifice (sword arm) for the greater well-being of all. The following is one version of the binding of Fenrir:

> They say that long ago, when the gods of Asgard and the gods of Vanaheim were at peace, the world of Midgard found its golden age. The goddesses of Wyrd, the three sisters known as the Norns, foretold

the end of the world...telling the all father, Woden, through the seer Voulspa.

Ragnarok, the end of the world, would be hastened by the children of Loki. Jormungandr was said to strike the world dead, poisoning the sky. Fenrir would devour all the gods, including Odin himself. And Helja would weave a shadow over the world, casting it into darkness eternal.

For this, the children must be disposed of. But Odin was not unwise and not a cruel man, though many would make such claims of the All-Father. He devised a plan to keep them all from the world itself and from the Ragnarok.

The three children of Loki and Angrbroda, Odin did summon:

Jormangandr, the great serpent, he threw within the ocean of Midgard. The serpent grew so large that it encompassed the world itself, biting its own tail. Odin knew that by doing this he would protect Midgard for many years to come from the accursed giants.

Hel, goddess of shadows, he banished her to the lands of Nifelheim. There she met the old goddess of death and life, Helga, and with her help learned the domains of the dead and living. It was from there that deep within the ice she would create a city where the dead could rest...Eljudinir. This domain would be where all in the nine worlds would come to be judged. Odin knew that by doing this, he had given the world further order to those who passed from old age, sickness, or from hard work. In her world, past the nine gates called Nagrind, the evil would be laid upon the frozen shores of her city and devoured by Niddhog, the chaos dragon, and the good would sleep until their next incarnation deep within her halls.

Fenrir, the great wolf lord, he gave to the god Tyr. For only Tyr was brave enough to feed and care for the "monster." Odin knew that by doing this perhaps the monster would be made friendly, and the love and strength of the god of warriors would instill discipline and honor in the creature.

Many years passed, but finally the wolf became too large for Tyr to handle. The great god, Fenrir, lord of the wolves, began to run across the lands of Midgard challenging all who would get into his way. Fenrir killed many gods and people alike.

Odin called his court together and asked of the gods to slay the great beast. But none dared to answer, for fear of the creature who could kill gods. But even if they had been brave enough to answer, none would...for in their midst sat Tyr, his eyes filled with tears. He looked up at the All-Father and announced himself, saying that he and only he would slay Fenrir...his once longtime friend.

But Tyr did not wish to kill the great wolf, and so he traveled to the Dvergar (the dwarves). With dwarven craft, Tyr drew forth the magical silver from the ground itself, made pure by the smith magic of the Volunder. He had them mine the special metal of magical silver known as Mithril. He then traveled to the Alfar (the elves). To them he requested many things: the sound of a cat's footfall, the beard of a woman, the roots of a mountain, bear's sinews, fish's breath, and bird's spittle. After gathering these, he took them to the great smith Wayland, and the ancient weapon smith of the gods forged him two magical chains: one named Loethinger, the other Dromi. With elven craft and with the ingredients gained from dwarf and elf, a cord was forged that they named Glipnir. Tyr wove the magical silver into a cord that nothing could break, not even a god...and it was from this gift, they say, that the great God Tyr would bind Fenrir himself.

Tyr traveled to the isle of Lyngiv in a lake called Amsvartnir, and there he faced the great wolf god. It was there that Tyr challenged the great wolf to the Holmgang (a battle of honor). But before these two great beings would do battle, Tyr wished to see great feats of strength, so that if the wolf god lost the Holmgang, Tyr would be able to tell his great deeds to the world.

Fenrir laughed at this but agreed to placate the warrior god, for he did not think that he would lose. The first challenge was that of Loethinger, a chain made of earth and fire. Fenrir tore this chain in twain easily. The second challenge was that of Dromi, a chain made of water and air. Fenrir tore this chain to shreds as well. The third challenge was that of Glipnir. Fenrir saw how thin the cord was...silver and thin, elven make yet of dwarven metal. He sensed a deception. He promised to take the challenge only if the warrior god promised to place his hand into the wolf's mouth...thus ensuring that Tyr would keep his word to free him if he was truly bound. Tyr agreed.

Tyr stood forth and placed his hand in the wolf's mouth, wrapping the loop around Fenrir's neck. Instantly, the god was bound, and he growled, demanding to be freed. Tyr refused the god, and thus his hand became forfeit. Tyr took the god wolf Fenrir to a place where he knew that he would never harm another, and sent him to live upon the moon. Tyr drove a silver pin deep within a stone called Gijoll. He buried this stone deep within the moon to the heart of it, called Thiviti, so that the wolf god could not leave. Tyr then thrust into his mouth a sword called Berkvai: the guards caught in his lower jaw, and the point in the upper. This became his gag. He howled hideously, and slaver ran out of his mouth: This formed a river that is called Van; there he lies till the Twilight of the Gods.

To this day, we know that the wolf god Fenrir is tied to the moon, for the wolves of Midgard still howl in homage to their bound deity.[167]

This is only one version of the tale of Týr and Fenrir; there are many others. In all of the legends, there are numerous teachings hidden. "Many believe the Norse gods and the other mythological beings of ancient Scandinavia represent aspects of the self, our emotions, and the many qualities that make up the psyche of the human self."[168] For example, the most honorable of the gods, Týr, betrayed the trust of the wolf and broke a pledge to him. The result was that he lost his sword hand, very impactful for a god of war. What teaching does this reveal to you? Týr, god of justice and associated with heroic glory, demonstrates for us the need to sacrifice for natural justice—the well-being of all. This is not human-made law but the natural law of creation. Sacrifice is needed today to stop the destruction of the earth and its creatures. What are you willing to sacrifice?

In another example, *Fenrisúlfr* was one of Loki's offspring. On the surface, Loki is best known as a dark trickster, a god working from the dark side. However, his earliest-known identity was the god of the domestic hearth—the indispensable household fire, a fire that was constructive not destructive. Over time, the dark side of his personality takes over and we have Loki as the cunning liar and traitorous destroyer of innocence and righteousness. This aspect of self, where the light of an individual gradually slips into the dark, is a theme that happens more often than not to individuals, especially ones who are very creative in the arts. Since the dark is symbolic of our creative potential, a person's creative darkness may slowly become a destructive darkness, e.g., drugs, alcohol, and so forth, to feed the "beast."

Furthermore, Fenrir, the son of Loki, is symbolic of the destructive dark within us. But Loki had a constructive as well as a destructive side. Would not the Fenrir wolf also have a hidden constructive side to his darkness, just like his father? This is a question to ponder. All of this points us to one conclusion: Fenrisúlfr is our metaphoric beast within.

Beast Within

> Blessed is the wolf which the man eats and the wolf
> will become man; and cursed is the man whom the
> wolf eats and the wolf will become man.[169]

There is an ancient cross-cultural concept referred to as the "beast within." The beast is most commonly portrayed as either a lion or a wolf. It symbolizes the untamed nature of our primitive or hindbrain, where instincts such as survival, dominance, and mating are located. Metaphorically then, our beast is an inner quality that is intimately connected with our issues of safety, security, survival, and sex. All humans have a fierceness and ferociousness within them—the beast within. Consciously, many people ignore this quality of self; many fear it, while others deny it totally. But our inner beast is neutral. It is not, by its nature, solely a positive or a negative quality. One way to think of our beast is as the sum total of our strength, willpower, and sexual potency. These are important qualities that we need in our lives in order to be fully human, fully healthy, and fully energetic.

However, these qualities and others may be turned negative or destructive through such things and emotions like denial, madness, anger, rage, substance abuse, revenge, envy, hate, jealousy, and fear. Add to this list power, greed, and control over others, and it's easy to see the potential of unleashing the dysfunctional and destructive, dark qualities of our beast.

Too often, we forget that without the dark, there would be no light. Our lives are usually organized into a separation between the symbolic light and symbolic dark, with the light held up as our ultimate goal in spiritual and religious life. The true secret that most never realize is that light and dark are equal components that interpenetrate. True spiritual and religious teachings are based on the acknowledgment of the interpenetrative aspect of dark and light within us and then the growth of our light or the divine aspect of our soul from the creative darkness of our humanity.

This is not the Jungian concept of the shadow but the actual and physical reality of dualistic concepts that interpenetrate. The dualistic light and dark is the illusion, as our individual sense of reality (of separateness or duality) is an extension of the illusion of our basic core sense perceptions. Our eyes perceive separation between ourselves and all things viewed. This constant reinforcement tricks us into thinking and believing that we are separate and an island unto ourselves.

The reality is that we are not separate at all but deeply interconnected. My philosophy is based on the concept of nondifferentiating knowledge. Its foundation is interpenetrating radical nonduality—oneness. There is no separation between the absolute and the relative, dark and light, spirit and matter, or mind and body. The most profound and essential nature of things is not distinct from the things recognizable by our senses.

Similarly, our symbolic light and dark are not separate but interpenetrate to define our wholeness as individuals. Additionally, the two sides of our inner darkness also interpenetrate. There is no separate shadow, just a darkness that is both creative and destructive at the same time.

The shadow is considered an archetype by Jungians[170] and connected with the unconscious, but Jung advanced no connection to physiological reality. With the concept of the dark, there is a connection to the body—testosterone. This hormone is our bodily source of physical strength, willpower, and sexual potency. Testosterone is the source of our beast within.

This important hormone is made in large amounts by the testicles. But testosterone is not limited solely to men. Women produce testosterone in their ovaries, even though it is only about one-tenth of what a male produces, just as a male produces a small amount of the female hormone estrogen. Additionally, both men and women produce a small amount of testosterone in their adrenal glands, which are the source of our fight-or-flight mechanism—a reaction of our beast. But "the modern, technological world gives us few positive outlets for this energy, and yet the pressures of our lives are constantly causing our bodies to send us hormonal messages to fight or flee."[171]

⚜

The beast within, ignored or turned negative, is the root cause of the seemingly ever-present abuse issues found within all levels and stratums of society. Abuse is not solely limited to physical actions. The untamed beast is literally ignorance running rampant. Ignorance, not to be equated to educational level or intelligence, is solely a materialistic, dualistic view of life, which results in a spiritually unawakened consciousness. This ignorance then inflates and protects the unhealthy ego's sense of survival, resulting in arrogance. This arrogance, in turn, feeds the untamed beast. This is the very same arrogance that turns a blind eye to all forms of abuse, especially if reporting or stopping the abuse would threaten the person's external power or position in the world.

The beast wants to constantly feed its source of power.[172] Particularly, the beast is the source of dysfunctional sexual behavior. These are not sexual issues that the church rules as dysfunctional, such as homosexuality, but dysfunctional sexual behaviors that harm another individual, such as pedophilia, rape, and incest. It can also manifest in the manipulation of another through sex for power, control, or influence.

It is important to understand that the beast lies within each of us, male and female alike. As much as we may want to deny our beast within, doing so would be denying our own sources of physical strength and potency. Our denial of the dark leaves our light in a vulnerable position—in its so-called sole existence of truth. The dark is symbolic of our creative potential, a quality we would not want to destroy or inhibit. Additionally, denial may lead to a consciousness of passive victimization. Metaphorically, our sword arm is impotent and cut off.

On the other hand, denying the beast within may allow it de facto permission to run wild in our spirits, feeding and perpetrating a wasteland within us and outside us in the process. The Roman Catholic Church is guilty of this denial. Look at how its denial has manifested in the world—vulnerable children abused. But to shift the blame, the Church provides a substitute for the beast in the guise of the devil—the devil made me do it. In an interview, the previous pope, Pope Benedict XVI, "acknowledged some of the church's failings, like in the sexual-abuse crisis, which he called 'a volcano of filth' sent by the devil."[173]

❧

We must bind or slay our beast through the process of transmutation—in other words, tame and awaken our beast within. This will transform it into an inner quality of altruistic strength, divine willpower, and altruistic sexual potency—love as profane and sacred sexuality. These are the qualities that are based on love, not on fear, control, manipulation, or revenge. We still possess the power of the beast, but it is tamed and will work for our benefit and the benefit of the earth and humanity. This is the strength and power to awaken our hearts and inner sparks while defending the downtrodden. No longer do we express excessive aggression nor have the impulse or need to abuse or destroy other people or other things.

❖

The Norse-Germanic people viewed the beast two ways, reflected by the "two words *vargr* (Anglo-Saxon *vearg*) and *úlfr* (Anglo-Saxon *vulf*); vargr is the demon beast, and no man could be vargr unless he was bereft of frith, given over to trolls and roving beastlike in the woods; wolf, on the other hand, is a friend of the king, and his name is often borne among men. To be true to the ancient sense, we had perhaps better say that language needed two words, because there were two beings: the animal that enters into league with man, and the wild beast of the trolls. The use of Wolf as a title of honor for warriors and as a man's name, and still more the existence of *Ylfing* or *Vylfing* as a family name, implies that men might overcome the strangeness of the animal and draw it into a firm alliance; such wolf-men surely had wolf nature: the strength of a wolf and part of his habits."[174]

❖

As we can see, the wolf symbolizes our beast within. If the wolf stays unawakened (spiritually) and untamed (mentally and physically), our first chakra[175] actions and behaviors may be dysfunctional and possibly abusive. This is the unhealthy ego, seeing reality only from the "I" and seeing issues of security, basic needs, survival, profane sex, inappropriate sexual activity, and one's sense of roots, family, and connection to the earth and nature as hostile. In other words, the wolf has eaten the man; "the wolf will become man—vargr (demon beast)," and the man is cursed. However, if we awaken the altruistic power of the wolf, we have symbolically eaten the wolf instead of the wolf eating us. We are blessed, not cursed; "and the wolf will become man—úlfr." Being blessed is metaphorically the equivalent of achieving the healthy ego, where reality is based on the "I" in the "we" and the "we" in the "I."

Metaphorically, our wolf (power and fierceness), now tamed, has not eaten the sheep but has lain down with the sheep (showing compassion and gentleness). The wolf and sheep are one. With the focus of our wolf power now on compassionately creating and not furiously destroying, we are able to journey into the unknown with gentle power and face our fears with compassion. Furthermore, we achieve a state where the use of power is balanced. This is the ability to know when to let our wolf howl, when to let it be silent, and when to unleash its power.

When we tame the beast within, we become responsible for our actions and our behaviors. The key is the relationship of self and other—being responsible and caring means that we will not consciously hurt anyone else through our actions.

However, we do not metaphorically become saints. We still have basic, primal survival, safety, and sexual wants and needs. Through the process of taming our beasts, we are able to let go of some of our destructive behaviors but not all. When we don't let them go, we symbolically press them down or bind them. Keep in mind that Óðinn is a Binder God. Look to Óðinn to assist you in binding any destructive wolf behaviors that are still at work within you. Týr gave his sword arm; what are you willing to sacrifice to tame and/or bind your beast?

Pressing Down or Binding

I believe in an interpenetration of all aspects of reality. This means the darkness that we have within us has both constructive and destructive sides. They are not separate but interpenetrate. In other words, even if we awaken our beast within, we have not separated our constructive side from our destructive side. The destructive side is still there and could at some future time rear its ugly head. This is one of the times where pressing down or binding comes in handy.

This means keeping inappropriate actions and behaviors under control. This is not an act of suppression. It just means that one is not acting on or repeating destructive behaviors.

There are dysfunctional and possibly destructive emotions, behaviors, and thought processes that, with work, we are able to let go of or transform. But ours is not a dualistic either-or reality. There will be ones that can't be transformed. Instead, they need to be pressed down or bound. This means keeping inappropriate first chakra actions and behaviors under control, where they are still there but are never acted upon.

Berserkers and Wolfskins—Unleashing the Beast

A common image of a berserker is one of a naked, wrathful warrior who had such battle lust and a trancelike fury that they bit their shields. Covering their nakedness may be the skin of a bear or a wolf.

According to Lars Magnar Enoksen, Master of Glima (Viking fighting), the Viking warriors had "the advantage of being able to bring forth the rage of the mighty bear and the deadly wolf. This inhuman state of mind is regarded as being given from the warrior god and magician Óðinn or 'the one that is inspired by rage' and is called *Berserksgangr* or 'to go berserk.' The warriors who are able to go into this God-given state of mind are known as the Berserkers."[176]

Lars is correct in labeling the berserker condition as an inhuman (beast) state of mind. Past scholars have attempted to equate the berserker state with a state of religious ecstasy or one achieved through the use of magic mushrooms. It has been suggested "that berserks used a poisonous mushroom, fly agaric, to arouse themselves,"[177] even though there is no mention of such drugs in the sagas; there doesn't appear to be any evidence to support this.

There is some supposition that "at the end of the ninth century, some warriors were still called *berserkir* (the word is probably old). They either resembled or were identical with úlfheðnar 'wolfcoats.' Both groups roared and howled when they fought. They may have worn animal masks, but this need not be the reason they were called *berserkir* and *úlfheðnar*."[178]

The most primitive form of masking is simply the painting of the face and/or body. Face painting delves deeper than masking within our consciousness by unlocking the quality or qualities we are bonding with in a transformation from our mundane selves into supernatural selves. I know the power of this process, as I have had a vision, conferred by Vince Stogan, on painting my face for increased spiritual power (my face paint is a reflection of my hamingja). In Vince's tradition and in other shamanic beliefs, you must have a vision, confirmed by a traditional indigenous shaman, before you can paint your face. You cannot just make something up.

⚜

According to Anatoly Liberman the later concept of the berserker, at least in part, may have been birthed by homeless, unmarried men who were no longer "going Viking":

> When the activity of the Vikings came to an end, professional soldiers lost their occupation and status and degenerated into riffraff preying on farmers. The plundering rabble of the Icelandic sagas is fact, not fiction. The near-formulaic nature of the episodes notwithstanding, bands of able-bodied men in their prime, unused to agricultural pursuits and trade, wandered all over Scandinavia and made life of farming communities miserable. Earl Eiríkr Hákonarson outlawed berserks in 1012, as is told in chapter 19 of Grettis saga, and this may have been the reason they migrated to other countries, including Iceland. The Icelandic Jus Ecclesiasticum (1123) and the law code Grágás made berserks subject to the lesser outlawry...
>
> The homeless, unmarried men in their prime were not sweet tempered. Many of them became psychopaths, flying into rages at the slightest provocation. When thwarted, they immediately lost control of themselves. Shield biting and the rest were part of a well-rehearsed performance...Feigning hysteria is a dangerous game; its symptoms become the actor's second nature.[179]

Whatever the origin of the berserker, their state of mind is most important to us. The berserker demonstrates the ability of certain individuals to willingly release their beasts within. I doubt if there was much attempt in taming it so its power would be focused on constructive ends, not destructive ones. However, keep in mind that the beast released may be constructive in its rage, to prevent the slaughter of innocents by the slaughter of ones who would prey on the weak, but the killing of others is still involved. This concept of the beast within is very important in awakening the power of our hearts. Please ponder this concept and answer the question: In what state is your beast? Unawakened, out of control, or awakened? If unawakened or out of control, what do you need to do to awaken it by transmutation and the binding of certain behaviors?

Óðinn's Einherjar

Einherjar is a slippery concept to say the least. Traditionally, they are known as the chosen ones taken to Valhöll, where they fight during the day, are resurrected to drink and feast, and then repeat this sequence day after day. Supposedly they are preparing to assist Óðinn at the end times of Ragnarok. According to Gunnar Viking Ólafsson, jarl of the Einherjar Vikings of Reykjavík, "*Einherjar Vikings* means 'army of one,' and Oðin means 'the one.' They are Oðin's army. The group's mission is 'to show tribute to the Vikings and other warriors alike so they may never be forgotten.'"[180] I feel that Gunnar is opening the window on these dead heroes in Óðinn's Valhöll. All things considered, it seems that we may be dealing with a mythic paradigm of elite warrior societies or brotherhoods. This paradigm is needed today. But how do we achieve this?

Keep in mind that this is not a Reconstructionist manual. However, with an underlying acceptance of deeds not words, I believe the following knowledge is important in helping each of us become more powerful in heart and mind. This will assist us with our deeds of life.

It is generally accepted that the Einherjar are the "dead heroes of Valhöll." They are also known as Óðinn's "one-harriers." These are champions—elite warriors. According to Elsa-Brita Titchenell's *The Masks of Odin*:

> All mythologies contain some tales of the struggle of a hero, his trials, and either failure or success in overcoming obstacles—the echoes of his own past—to reunite with his divine self...
>
> The sagas which relate the trials of the initiate are the most popular and best known of all stories and legends, even in exoteric literature, though seldom recognized as such. In these adventure stories the hero must first become totally fearless for himself; he must wrest from the "dragon" of wisdom the secrets of "birdsong": this means he

must know at firsthand the structure and functions of the universe; he must be willing to sacrifice all personal ambition, even his own soul's success, to an all-encompassing concern for the welfare of the whole. One who succeeds in attaining such selfless universality becomes a coworker with the gods, a beneficent force powerfully impelling the evolvement of the world in which he is a component.

The fabled home of the Edda's elect, where the heroes go after being killed in battle, is Valhalla...Valhalla is protected by many barriers: it is surrounded by a moat, Tund, wherein a werewolf, Tjodvitner, fishes for men. Its gate is secured by magic, and on the door of the hall a wolf hangs transfixed, surmounted by a blood-dripping eagle. In addition it is guarded by Odin's two wolfhounds. To understand the significance of all this we must define the terms used.

Each of the barriers to the Hall of the Elect is symbolic of some weakness that must be conquered. The warrior who would cross the river of time (Tund) and the river of doubt (Ifing) must maintain unwavering purpose and self-direction if he is not to be swept away by the turbulent currents of temporal existence. He must evade the bestial cravings of his animal nature (the lures of Tjodvitner) if he is to gain the other shore...

Next, the candidate seeking Valhalla must overcome the hounds Gere (greed) and Freke (gluttony): he must avoid desire, even the desire for the wisdom he is seeking, if he is to obtain it. To find the secret of the magic gate, he must have strength of aspiration, purity of motive, and inflexible resolve. The wolf and the eagle must be vanquished and transfixed over the entrance to the hall to guard against their intrusion. This means conquering the bestial nature (the wolf), and pride (the eagle)...

The candidate for universality cannot, by the very nature of his quest, regard himself as separate from the whole; he can therefore have no use for divisive means of any kind, in thought, word, or deed. First to go are weapons of offense, as harmlessness is cultivated. Thereafter all means of defense are dropped and finally all personal protection of whatever kind. The one-harrier has stepped beyond the notion of separateness. His work lies not in the immediate but in the eternal. He is no longer bounded by a self but extends unlimited; the hero soul has discarded all personal concern, placing complete reliance on the divine law he unconditionally serves...[181]

This rendition and explanation of the concept of Einherjar may not be historically correct. On the other hand, it may have been an underlying mind-set of some of the Norse warriors, where they understood the destructiveness of doubt and their need to overcome it or press it down. And as we have already discussed, an elite warrior would have conquered their bestial nature, so they had the ability to let it loose when it was necessary and to control it, so as not to "feed the ravens."

Ravens

Óðinn's companions, ravens and wolves, are both connected in folklore and in reality. Ravens, "wolf birds," have a social attachment with wolves, sometimes playfully teasing the wolves and at other times eating their leftovers. It seems that they have a close relationship that is beneficial to both. Of course, both are viewed as scavengers of the battlefield.

Óðinn's ravens have a unique identity and purpose and could be considered direct extensions of him, of his mind (divine consciousness). On his shoulders sit his two ravens Huginn (Old Norse for "thought mind") and Muninn (Old Norse for the "thought memory"); these birds of battle are also symbolic of flights in search of knowledge and wisdom. Turville-Petre believes "Huginn and Muninn must be seen as Óðinn's spiritual qualities in concrete form. A man's fetch, appearing in the guise of an animal, is sometimes called *hugr*."[182]

As a battle bird, the raven image was famously captured through the raven banners of the Jarls of Orkney and the sons of Ragnarr Loðbrók. They were regarded as totemic objects of magical power. "Icelandic sources also mention a magical raven banner. This was called *Hrafnsmerki*, and is described in the *Orkneyinga Saga*, *Þorsteins Saga Síðu-Hallssonar*, and in *Njáls Saga*."[183]

❧

Air is commonly symbolic of our mind just as fire is symbolic of our spirit. Birds carry the same symbolic identity as air and therefore mind. Many times, birds are symbolic of the divine mind or consciousness. This is illustrated when the hero Sigurðr tastes the dragon's blood and immediately gains wisdom and knows the language of birds—angelic or divine language.

As we know, ravens and Valkyrjur are closely associated with Óðinn. According to Timothy Bourns in *The Language of Birds in Old Norse Tradition*, "The Valkyrjur are reminiscent of the human figures who comprehend bird speech. The Valkyrja in *Hrafnsmál* is wise and thus able to converse with a bird; in turn, the raven offers information about worldly people and events. The association with kingship is equally obvious. The entire poem is in praise of a king and his deeds."[184]

Óðinn is "able to understand the speech of birds, specifically the ravens Huginn and Muninn; and a god transformed into the shape of a bird, who spits the mead of poetry from his mouth—a clear form of bird speech in highly mythicized form."[185] The bird Óðinn transformed into was the eagle. In his quest for the mead of poetry, Óðinn shape changed into a serpent and crawled into the mountain, where the mead was kept. "While inside, he sleeps with Gunnlöð for three nights, the same amount of time that Sigurðr sleeps with Brynhildr in *Völsunga saga*." Óðinn then transforms into an eagle, flying away with the sacred mead of inspiration.

What we have in this myth of the thief of the mead of poetry is a guide to initiation and the awakening of wisdom. The serpent and bird are common motifs in this process. Traditionally, the serpent represents the first chakra issues such as profane sex, as witnessed by Óðinn's sex with the jötunn (gaint), Gunnlöð. The eagle may represent a divine state, whereas the serpent is the human state. Combined, they are the feathered serpent or the divine human whose consciousness is with the gods—the wisdom of divine consciousness.

Óðinn—Allfather of Wisdom and God of Poets, Magic, and Runes

As the Allfather of wisdom, Óðinn "acquired much of his wisdom from his giant relatives, and particularly from the wise giant Vafthrúðnir. Vafthrúðnir could tell the secrets of the giants and of all the gods, for he had traveled through all the nine worlds; he had even penetrated Niflhel, into which men pass from the world of death (Hel), as if dying for a second time."[186]

From Hliðskjálf, his high-seat, Óðinn sees all and knows all but still wanders the realms, like Vafthrúðnir, ever seeking knowledge and power by speaking to wise people, such as prophets and philosophers, and listening to the music of the wilds, the sounds of nature. This trait of wandering is necessary to accumulate knowledge and the wisdom that may flow from it. When was the last time you wandered through the forests and mountains? When did you leave the comfort of your home country and wander into the unknown of a foreign land? Were you alone in your wandering, like Óðinn? Much power and wisdom comes from this. It is the source of inspiration for poets—no need for excessive ale or drug-induced inspiration.

As wandering seekers, much magic may be revealed to us and inspire us. Nature will speak to us if our hearts are open and our minds are still. Magic (the power of nature) is alive, but are you aware?

Power—Seiðr and Galdr

Once again, we have entered a twisted landscape, seeking truth. Is it in the valley, on the mountaintop, possibly behind that rock? My approach in determining a path through the twists and turns of the scholarly and archeological information is my direct Northwest Coast shamanic knowledge, practice, experience, and my esoteric Buddhist knowledge and practice of what would be identified as seiðr and galdr. Even though the scholarly approach is to separate these two concepts, I combine them as intertwining aspects of mystical, magical, otherworldly "work"—in other words, what is commonly known as magic and sorcery. Keep in mind that sorcery does not equate black magic. Once again, when life is viewed through a prism of dualism, then things may be labeled as good or bad, white or black. The truth is that there is no such thing as black magic or white magic. Magic is magic; power is power. It is the intent that determines whether magic is utilized for healing (white) or harming (black).

As a sign of the times, the terms *seiðr* and *galdr* are probably more appropriate than magic or sorcery. For the common person, both magic and sorcery paint a picture of stage magic, or negativity, in their minds. This is further exacerbated by disempowered people, who never put in the years of apprenticeship or extensive sacrifice self to self, claiming to be shamans, druids, wiccans, and so forth. The indigenous power workers, who I have apprenticed with over the decades, never referred to their powers as magic. The reason: in truth, the power exhibited is not out of the ordinary; it is ordinary; it is flowing through all things. It is Óðinn's unseen power of creation—seiðr. The difference is that the majority of people do not have the radical nondualistic consciousness, power, or strength of heart and mind to access it. But it is there—just feel the force of a storm or observe the beauty of a flower.

Let's explore this power. This power or "The Force"—the term George Lucas coined in in his *Star Wars* movies—is the single, dynamic, sacred power or energy that is the unifying totality of all things—a universal life force.[187] It's in constant movement, eternally self-generating and self-regenerating while encompassing and interpenetrating the whole cosmos. It is immanent and at the same time transcendent. This "Force" is only accessible through direct personal experience and must be awakened. There are seven aspects to this power:

1. Consciousness—the greatest power is only accessible through a consciousness of radical nonduality. This force must be awakened. However, a small amount of power is accessible through a dualistic consciousness.
2. Knowledge—a correct perception of reality. Knowledge is wisdom about the true nature of things, the capacity to see with our hearts.
3. Fate—power is consistent with one's inner nature. It can be sought, but seeking does not guarantee that one will attain it.
4. Individuality—only comes to ones who are ready or worthy through sacrificing self to self.
5. Variability—everyone has some power, but its amount and intensity vary from person to person. It must be acquired through strenuous effort, though fate will determine its acceptance.
6. Sacrificing Self to Self—Óðinn illustrates this concept of acquiring and accumulating power through the strenuous effort of sacrificing self to self.
7. Intrinsic—power permeates everything; however, in certain individuals, certain objects, and certain natural locations, power is more focused and intense.

This power on a personal level is the inner heat generated by the shaman. Interesting enough, the feeling is one of icy fire. The first time I experienced it coursing through my body, I thought I was having a heart attack. This is the power of creation as witnessed by the Norse creation myth of the blending of fire and ice.

✦

Combined with the intertwining relationship of seiðr and galdr is the realization that the isolation of seiðr practitioner as female and galdr as male is problematic. Originally, *seiðr* meant "custom" or "tradition," which was the province of females. However, the practice of seiðr as magic and galdr as song indicates a person possessing otherworldly spirit power—the gender of the person is not important.

When discussing seiðr, a problem of identity usually occurs—is it the magical practice, or spells being used, or is it the force that gives power to the spell? Seiðr is both—the power and the practice or tradition. But what activates this power? The answer is the strength of the person's mind and galdr. This may be viewed as inner power plus vibration equals a force that defies materialistic reality. Matter is energy, and one of the most effective and efficient ways of affecting energy and matter is through the vibrational power of our voice. This does not necessarily mean a loud vocalization; a whisper may be just as effective. In fact, loud may be the least effective, depending on circumstances. Loud may stop an argument, but it will not get your point across as the other person's body will tense up. A tense body means a closed mind. This is the reason decision making needs to be done under physically relaxed, not tense or stressed, circumstances.

Moreover, there may be bodily actions and movement, such as walking counterclockwise, possibly backward, or arm/hand motions. In the Icelandic *Vatnsdæla saga*, Bárðr, a male power worker, is "requested to break a spell of bad weather. The account then tells how: 'He asked them to join arms and form a circle; he then walked around widdershins[188] three times and spoke Irish; he asked them to agree to chant their approval. They did so. Then he waved a goatskin towards the mountain and the weather calmed down.'"[189] Walking around a circle of people counterclockwise, or counter sunwise, is the opening to the otherworld, which blends with our materialistic world. Three is the number symbolizing the divine or spirit world (otherworld). Since Bárðr is not Irish, "speaking Irish" may not have meant the Irish language, as many chants and songs have no actual linear meaning. Finally, the waving of the goatskin would be symbolic of requesting Þórr's aid in calming the weather. Waving of the goatskin toward the mountain would indicate the direction of the stormy weather that he was attempting to calm. The goatskin would have been one of Bárðr's power objects.

⚜

People of power such as shamans may be termed "*galdra smiðir,* 'smiths of in-cantations.'"[190] The traditional view of a smith is the blacksmith or swordsmith. What they both have in common is fire. Fire is a transformational agent that can turn raw iron into a sword. Water is also used by the smithy in the transfor-mational process. Our bodies are mostly composed of water and, when com-bined with our inner heat and the power of our voice, magic happens.

One of the Old Norse words for "spell, incantation"[191] is *galdr,* "derived from a word for singing incantations."[192] One of the most recognizable incan-tations is *abracadabra.* In Aramaic, the phrase is *avra kehdabra.* The chant is as follows: aaa-raaa-kaaa-daaa-raaa (*a* pronounced *ah*). It means "I create as I speak (resonate)." Galdr, singing incantation or song, is fundamental to rites of transformation and assessing power. In shamanic cultures, galdr is referred to as a "spirit song." These are quested for and intrinsically unique to the in-dividual shaman. However, there are set songs to accomplish such things as opening a stream or river for the rite of sacrificing self to self of bathing. In the Northwest Coast tradition, the quest is for four consecutive days. My wife and I both carry a spirit song. I assisted Vince Stogan once when a few people were questing for a song. None received a song. As I stated: "Fate: power, is consis-tent with one's inner nature. It can be sought, but seeking does not guarantee that one will attain it."

The most commonly recognized song of spirit or spell songs are Óðinn's. His spell songs are recorded in Hávamál and begin with stanza 146: "I know those spells no noble wife knows or the son of any man. One is called 'help,' and it will help you against strife and sorrow and every grief."[193] The spells end with stanza 163: "I know an eighteenth, which I never tell a maid or any man's wife: much better if only one is aware (the last it is of my chants), except only her my arms enfold, or perhaps my sister."[194] Óðinn's spells only tell us the pur-pose of the spell. The song that activates the spell is not revealed, as this knowl-edge of power would only be orally taught.

For many people, the most recognizable section of Hávamál is the one that precedes Óðinn's spell songs—his sacrifice self to self on Yggdrasill and his dis-covery of runes. "I know that I hung in the wind-torn tree Nine whole nights, spear-pierced, Consecrated to Odin, myself to my Self above me in the tree, Whose root no one knows whence it sprang. None brought me bread, none served me drink; I searched the depths, spied runes of wisdom; Raised them with song, and fell once more thence."[195] Once again, we see the importance and the need for a song of spirit—galdr.

One concluding point concerning Óðinn's sacrifice on Yggdrasill, it seems from the description that Óðinn is hanging upside down ("I searched the depths..."). This would indicate that a person seeking hidden knowledge would need to "inverse" their view of the world and reality as it is commonly viewed. Furthermore, in this head-down position the view is not of the sky but of the earth; the depths of the earth where the knowledge is hidden.

Runes

Runes and their use are not as straightforward as many authors would like you to believe. We are dealing with secret knowledge, a "hushed message."[196] Even though, "the term *rune* originally had two meanings: in Old English it could mean both 'runic letter' and 'secret' or 'knowledge,'"[197] I combine secret with knowledge as revealing the essence of the runes considering their association with magic. Additionally, there is a linkage between runes and galdr or magical songs, or in our case, "runic songs." In one sense, runes are magical writings. However, their origin is highly debatable and remains a matter of some controversy. Could runes have originated in nature, such as the figuration and variations of branches on a tree? A quick glance at the branches of a tree may reveal the runes *fehu, uruz, ansuz, gebo, isa, tiwaz,* and so forth. On the other hand, could the origins have been from striations on the sides of stony cliffs?

During one of my journeys to Norway, I was dealing with a disrespectful family causing disharmony within the group. I was staying in a home overlooking Gudvangen and Nærøyfjord. One morning, a steaming cup of coffee in hand, I walked outside to view the awesomeness of the sacred place. My eyes focused on the opposite cliff wall boarding the other side of the fjord and there was *fehu* clearly etched in the stone. My eyes slightly shifted as *uruz* was revealed and next to it was *nauðiz*—fun. Fun. Well, I was sure not having fun dealing with the dissention. But then again, the power of Gudvangen and the Norse lands spoke to me—have fun don't let a few bad apples spoil the beauty and power of the journey. Is this how the runes came into being? Maybe. But then again, my eyes have been trained to see differently, and possibly for that reason only, the spirits of the land said, "Have fun!"

⚜

The most recognizable of the different runic alphabets is the oldest the Elder Futhark so named for the first six letters of the runic alphabet, which has a total of twenty-four. I will not go into the meaning of each rune, as there are many books on the market. The key is to find which books that contain authentic knowledge and not the made-up stuff flowing from the unhealthy ego of an author.

Where there are runes, there are amulets and objects of power, such as a runic inscription on a sword or spearhead (magically imbued with the rune master's power). One spearhead from possibly the third century had the inscription *Ranja*, meaning 'router.' "The spear may seem, then, to have been thought to invoke fear in whoever faced its bearer in battle. But a nickname 'Router,' literally 'causes to run (away),' could, of course, equally have applied to its owner."[198] As we can see, the runic meaning is not straightforward.

Moreover, "runic inscriptions can be written from left-to-right (dextroverse), from right-to-left (sinistroverse), or even vary between the two (a practice called *boustrophedon*). A runic inscription may even begin at the bottom of an object and scroll its way up, or read in another irregular manner."[199] This is another example of how deciphering the meaning of runes is not so simple or straightforward. Add to this the use of treelike symbols that pertain to power, activating the force of the inscription, and that runes may be reversed.

⚜

When we discuss runic force or magic, we are presented with three seemingly important runic words—*alu*, *laþu*, and *laukaz*. All three seem to be charm words. The word *alu* has generally been accepted as meaning ale. It "reflects a word which originally described a religious or mystical state of mind, which was semantically transferred to a substance (fermented drink) used in religious and magical ritual. *Alu* becomes *öl* in Old Norse. Because *alu* so often comes at the end of magico-religious formulas, it seems rather clear that it was a verbal-symbolic formula used to conclude a sacred or magically potent utterance and that it has the effect of sanctifying (or 'loading') the foregoing words—just as sacrificial ale could be poured on a stone to sanctify it in religious ceremonies, which is especially known from funerary rites."[200]

Alu typically ends the formulas while *laþu* and *laukaz* many times formally begins the mystical invocations—*laþu* (formula or mystical phrase) *alu*. *Laþu* and *laukaz* could also be used together, such as was found on a golden pendant from Scania, southern Sweden: "'*Laþu, laukaz, gakaz, alu.*' 'Invocation, leek, cackle, dedication.' The term *gakaz* is an imitative word…It is often connected with a word for the cuckoo derived from an imitation of the noise that bird makes, but it seems more likely given the other imitative parallels that it also refers to a battle roar or the like. The term *leek* here might be supposed to indicate that the pendant is a fertility or amatory amulet, though, and that the votive terms *laþu* and *alu* are just generic charm words. But then 'leek' could also indicate (sexual) potency here, making the amulet a powerful warrior charm."[201] Keep in mind, that once again, it is the power within the individual that activates the power of the pendant. However, the pendant may help an individual overcome doubt, which will increase his or her power. Everything is intrinsic according to the circumstances and the interconnectedness of all things.

Continuing on, there is an inscription on a small runic stick from Swedish Lödöse (second half of the thirteenth century) that reads: "*Gordin, gordan; et gordan; ufau, ufai, ufao.*"[202] It is interesting to note that there is an ancient Hawaiian religious breathing exercise using vowels: *O piha ū, o piha ā, o piha ē, o piha ō*. There is a certain way to chant. How would you chant each one? What do you make of all of this?

Humanity Needs a Return to a Green Philosophy

Earth is a paradise of wonders all wrapped up in colors of blue and green. It is alive with a consciousness that responds to all the things that call it home. The Earth, Freyja's paradise, is under assault by the intrinsic evil of Capitalism fueled ever more by the dogma and doctrines of the Church. No matter the words of PR Pope Francis' Encyclical, dogma and doctrine will not change. Many people want to hear the words within his encyclical, but the bottom line is that there will be no change in the doctrine of the church concerning nature and its subservient position to "man." A change in doctrine to match the pope's encyclical would be to declare as doctrine the sacredness or divinity and consciousness of nature—until then, it is just the illusionary words of a hypocritical pope and the Church. Let the pope clean up the Vatican and its bank before falsely projecting his concern for the earth—our great Mother.

⚜

Hardly a day goes by without the media presenting some grim new findings as to how the world's ecological environment is on the brink of imploding and that if there isn't a radical and immediate change in how we think and live our lives on this planet then Doomsday is a mere few decades down the road.

Two major contributing factors as to why we seem so complacent about these constant warnings are firstly how divorced an ever-growing urbanized world has become from the natural environment and secondly our increasing failure to nurture an inner spiritual self.

For centuries Christianity preached that Man was the supreme ruler and the earth's resources were his for the taking. This Christian worldview encouraged Europe's aggressive drive to dominate and exploit nature in a spirit of complete indifference. With the bible in one hand and a sword or gun in the other, indigenous peoples were conquered, empires built and the Western world rode the wave of the Industrial Revolution and so-called progress. Granted, industrialization brought many advances, but it all came at a terrible price, both to the environment and that existentialist sense of soullessness that so often haunts us in the first world.

Science and technology alone are not going to get us out of the present ecological mess; we need to reconnect spiritually with the larger whole of reality. Unfortunately mainstream institutionalized religions seem incapable of offering such a holistic perspective; however many ancient indigenous religions do and we should be looking to them for ideas and inspiration. As the Yale scholar John Grim states: Indigenous peoples are ecologists and purveyors of an environmental wisdom absent in the technologically developed, industrialized "first world."[203]

⚜

Life doesn't occur inside the bubble anymore but inside a box! Science and organized religion separated us from nature, but now, technology has separated us from not only nature but each other. The illusion is connectivity, but the reality is isolation—we are boxes unto ourselves. When was the last time you had a conversation with someone heart to heart and eye to eye that lasted more than thirty minutes? When was the last time you sat and listened to the wind blowing through the trees while watching a bee settle its love on a flower? When was the last time you looked up at the cloud-filled sky's radiant white and blue?

There is great value in the world. Our world of everyday experience is the world of the divine. They are not separate. The cry of a raven is the sound of the divine. The daily chorus of beauty freely given to us by the winged ones reflects the heavenly music of the spheres. Our ordinary world provides us with an ongoing message of beauty, of spirit. But we need to listen—with quiet minds and hearts.

Nature is wondrous, a precious gem to embrace, and one not to be found within your smartphone or iPad. Your choice—wake up to the beauty of nature and each other, or stay asleep in a self-contained, secure illusion of life.

⚜

The rich source of creation and the mysteries of life are encoded in the pulse of each moment of our lives. As I write this, I can feel the holy blood streaming throughout my body, bringing the breath of life to every part of my soul. Stop for a moment and allow yourself to feel each of your senses: Feel the air that brushes your skin—feel it as it enters your body and nourishes your blood. How does this air taste? Look around and focus your eyes on the colors surrounding you; open your ears to the music of the earth and nature that is available to you. Now, close your eyes, and with each breath experience a moment of sacredness, holiness, divinity, the gift of life. Life is precious and not to be wasted in a wasteland of our own doing.

Each one of us, you and I, can transform our wasteland into a paradise on earth—a return to a green philosophy. We can achieve peace on earth and a oneness of humanity where we all share equally in all things and view each other as brother and sister. And we will discover that the world is truly an enchanted place where nature speaks to us and we can truly know our own intrinsic place in the symphony of life.

Begin now to awaken and help us return a green philosophy to the peoples of the earth. Let the world see and know the wisdom of Óðinn, the power of Þórr, and Freyja's power of nature.

APPENDIX

Be Uncivilized

Humanity needs a new story—a new myth. The destructiveness caused by the old myth is evident in the collapsing infrastructure of both society and the biosphere. The old consciousness will not right the wrongs that have been perpetrated for thousands of years.

People's attention has been focused on a flawed story (original sin, materialism, domination of nature, etc.) and an illusionary dream of 'mankind.' The attention needs to shift to a different one, a new story of equality, truth, power to the people and power to the earth—an egalitarian reality, not only for humankind, but for all things of the earth. This new story will give a different perspective of ourselves, the world around us and the things that we value.

Our new story is based on our hearts, not on our minds. It values the human family not the industrial elites. It sees value in partnership not exploitation of nature. It feels the bond between humanity and the earth not between 'man and money.' It hears a song of love not a sermon of greed and power. It tastes clean, clear water not industrial runoff. It smells the fragrant air not toxic emissions. Our human story values and recognizes the equality and worth of all living things of the earth and heaven. Our story values the wealth found within our hearts of compassion and love not the wealth of money and material things.

Our new myth begins with our continuing existence in the Garden of Eden sharing this paradise equally with all living things of the earth—an egalitarian existence. Our myth contains humanity's birth in original divinity not in original sin. Our myth awakens us to the knowledge that we are in partnership with all things of nature—we are one with nature not separate from it. We see each other in peace as brothers and sisters not in conflict as strangers or foes. We are no longer our brothers and sisters keeper; we are our brothers/sisters.

Our story goes on to portray us first and foremost as divine human beings by not segregating us into either male or female or different races. We see all life connected in a divine web of consciousness—where spirit and matter, the relative and the absolute interpenetrate in an oneness of being.

Uncivilization

I'm uncivilized. I feel one with nature not separate from it. I'm a wanderer adventuring through the hills, the valleys, the mountains, the jungles, across the shores and the seas of this world. Blessing, honoring, and respecting as I go—a part of nature not separate from it. I don't buy into "man's" superiority over nature, capitalism, capitalistic democracy, organized religion, corporate superiority, inequality, retirement, fear based first chakra issues, life longevity instead of life quality—short as life may be, and the list goes on-and-on. In other words I'm uncivilized. I haven't bought into the story of "man's" civilization. I am a stranger in a strange land. But only an uncivilized mind can see through the lie to the truth.

I envision an awakened egalitarian civilization spread throughout the width and breath of our beautiful earth. This is my nature of civilization—one of peace, kindness, love, forgiveness, equality, and oneness.

⚜

The following is excerpted from the manifesto of the Dark Mountain Project:[204]

> The myth of progress is founded on the myth of nature. The first tells us that we are destined for greatness; the second tells us that greatness is cost-free. Each is intimately bound up with the other. Both tell us that we are apart from the world; that we began grunting in the primeval swamps, as a humble part of something called 'nature', which we have now triumphantly subdued. The very fact that we have a word for 'nature' is evidence that we do not regard ourselves as part

of it. Indeed, our separation from it is a myth integral to the triumph of our civilisation. We are, we tell ourselves, the only species ever to have attacked nature and won. In this, our unique glory is contained.

Outside the citadels of self-congratulation, lone voices have cried out against this infantile version of the human story for centuries, but it is only in the last few decades that its inaccuracy has become laughably apparent. We are the first generations to grow up surrounded by evidence that our attempt to separate ourselves from 'nature' has been a grim failure, proof not of our genius but our hubris. The attempt to sever the hand from the body has endangered the 'progress' we hold so dear, and it has endangered much of 'nature' too. The resulting upheaval underlies the crisis we now face.

We imagined ourselves isolated from the source of our existence. The fallout from this imaginative error is all around us: a quarter of the world's mammals are threatened with imminent extinction; an acre and a half of rainforest is felled every second; 75% of the world's fish stocks are on the verge of collapse; humanity consumes 25% more of the world's natural 'products' than the Earth can replace — a figure predicted to rise to 80% by mid-century. Even through the deadening lens of statistics, we can glimpse the violence to which our myths have driven us.

And over it all looms runaway climate change. Climate change, which threatens to render all human projects irrelevant; which presents us with detailed evidence of our lack of understanding of the world we inhabit while, at the same time, demonstrating that we are still entirely reliant upon it. Climate change, which highlights in painful colour the head-on crash between civilisation and 'nature'; which makes plain, more effectively than any carefully constructed argument or optimistically defiant protest, how the machine's need for permanent growth will require us to destroy ourselves in its name. Climate change, which brings home at last our ultimate powerlessness....

We hear daily about the impacts of our activities on 'the environment' (like 'nature', this is an expression which distances us from the reality of our situation). Daily we hear, too, of the many 'solutions' to these problems: solutions which usually involve the necessity of urgent

political agreement and a judicious application of human technological genius. Things may be changing, runs the narrative, but there is
nothing we cannot deal with here, folks. We perhaps need to move
faster, more urgently. Certainly we need to accelerate the pace of research and development. We accept that we must become more 'sus-
tainable'. But everything will be fine. There will still be growth, there
will still be progress: these things will continue, because they have to
continue, so they cannot do anything but continue. There is nothing
to see here. Everything will be fine.

⚜

We do not believe that everything will be fine. We are not even sure,
based on current definitions of progress and improvement, that we
want it to be. Of all humanity's delusions of difference, of its separation from and superiority to the living world which surrounds it, one
distinction holds up better than most: we may well be the first species capable of effectively eliminating life on Earth. This is a hypoth-
esis we seem intent on putting to the test. We are already responsible for denuding the world of much of its richness, magnificence,
beauty, colour and magic, and we show no sign of slowing down.
For a very long time, we imagined that 'nature' was something that
happened elsewhere. The damage we did to it might be regrettable,
but needed to be weighed against the benefits here and now. And
in the worst case scenario, there would always be some kind of Plan
B. Perhaps we would make for the moon, where we could survive
in lunar colonies under giant bubbles as we planned our expansion
across the galaxy.

But there is no Plan B and the bubble, it turns out, is where we
have been living all the while. The bubble is that delusion of isolation
under which we have laboured for so long. The bubble has cut us off
from life on the only planet we have, or are ever likely to have. The
bubble is civilisation.

Consider the structures on which that bubble has been built. Its
foundations are geological: coal, oil, gas — millions upon millions

of years of ancient sunlight, dragged from the depths of the planet and burned with abandon. On this base, the structure stands. Move upwards, and you pass through a jumble of supporting horrors: battery chicken sheds; industrial abattoirs; burning forests; beam-trawled ocean floors; dynamited reefs; hollowed-out mountains; wasted soil. Finally, on top of all these unseen layers, you reach the well-tended surface where you and I stand: unaware, or uninterested, in what goes on beneath us; demanding that the authorities keep us in the manner to which we have been accustomed; occasion- ally feeling twinges of guilt that lead us to buy organic chickens or locally-produced lettuces; yet for the most part glutted, but not sated, on the fruits of the horrors on which our lifestyles depend....

⚜

If we are indeed teetering on the edge of a massive change in how we live, in how human society itself is constructed, and in how we relate to the rest of the world, then we were led to this point by the stories we have told ourselves — above all, by the story of civilisation.

This story has many variants, religious and secular, scientific, economic and mystic. But all tell of humanity's original transcendence of its animal beginnings, our growing mastery over a 'nature' to which we no longer belong, and the glorious future of plenty and prosperity which will follow when this mastery is complete. It is the story of human centrality, of a species destined to be lord of all it surveys, unconfined by the limits that apply to other, lesser creatures.

What makes this story so dangerous is that, for the most part, we have forgotten that it is a story. It has been told so many times by those who see themselves as rationalists, even scientists; heirs to the Enlightenment's legacy — a legacy which includes the denial of the role of stories in making the world.

Humans have always lived by stories, and those with skill in telling them have been treated with respect and, often, a certain wariness. Beyond the limits of reason, reality remains mysterious, as incapable of being approached directly as a hunter's quarry. With stories, with art, with symbols and layers of meaning, we stalk those elusive aspects of reality that go undreamed of in our philosophy. The storyteller weaves the mysterious into the fabric of life, lacing it with the comic, the tragic, the obscene, making safe paths through dangerous territory.

Yet as the myth of civilisation deepened its grip on our thinking, borrowing the guise of science and reason, we began to deny the role of stories, to dismiss their power as something primitive, childish, outgrown....

Yet for all this, our world is still shaped by stories. Through television, film, novels and video games, we may be more thoroughly bombarded with narrative material than any people that ever lived. What is peculiar, however, is the carelessness with which these stories are channelled at us — as entertainment, a distraction from daily life, something to hold our attention to the other side of the ad break. There is little sense that these things make up the equipment by which we navigate reality. On the other hand, there are the serious stories told by economists, politicians, geneticists and corporate leaders. These are not presented as stories at all, but as direct accounts of how the world is. Choose between competing versions, then fight with those who chose differently. The ensuing conflicts play out on early morning radio, in afternoon debates and late night television pundit wars. And yet, for all the noise, what is striking is how much the opposing sides agree on: all their stories are only variants of the larger story of human centrality, of our ever-expanding control over 'nature', our right to perpetual economic growth, our ability to transcend all limits.

⚜

Mainstream art in the West has long been about shock; about busting taboos, about Getting Noticed. This has gone on for so long that it has become common to assert that in these ironic, exhausted, post-everything times, there are no taboos left to bust. But there is one.

The last taboo is the myth of civilisation. It is built upon the stories we have constructed about our genius, our indestructibility, our manifest destiny as a chosen species. It is where our vision and our self-belief intertwine with our reckless refusal to face the reality of our position on this Earth. It has led the human race to achieve what it has achieved; and has led the planet into the age of ecocide. The two are intimately linked. We believe they must decoupled if anything is to remain.

⚜

We tried ruling the world; we tried acting as God's steward, then we tried ushering in the human revolution, the age of reason and isolation. We failed in all of it, and our failure destroyed more than we were even aware of. The time for civilisation is past. Uncivilisation, which knows its flaws because it has participated in them; which sees unflinchingly and bites down hard as it records — this is the project we must embark on now. This is the challenge for writing — for art — to meet. This is what we are here for.[205]

Be Uncivilized – Be an Earth Warrior in the Service of Þórr

Earth warriors are Þórr's warriors. If you wear Þórr's hammer, consider yourself an earth warrior defending Freyja, Freyr, and Njörðr's paradise from the destructive forces of Christianity and Capitalism. Begin now, recruit others, stop the destruction and pollution, spread the word, and return a green philosophy to humanity.

Rev. Dr. JC Husfelt

Rev. Dr. JC Husfelt, author of *I Am a Sun of God and So Are You*, *The Return of the Feathered Serpent*, and *Do You Like Jesus—Not the Church?*, is a philosopher, shaman, and mystic as well as a poet, martial artist, visionary, and exemplary prophet.

Since 1964, Husfelt has undertaken a literal and metaphorical journey through the mystical and practical aspects of the martial arts, mystery, myth, and spiritual lore of indigenous cultures throughout the world. He and his wife have traveled across the Americas to the icy plateaus and volcanoes of Iceland, through the windswept barrens of the British Isles and the Orkneys, and across Norway, Europe, the Mediterranean, Asia, and the Polynesian Islands.

Husfelt's teachings grew from his firsthand experience with multiple cultures and their spirituality. For more information, please e-mail him at bigcatthatflies@gmail.com or visit any of his websites:

www.divinehumanity.com
www.revolutioninreligion.com
www.spartanwarriorphilosophers.com

NOTES

1. In October of 1993, my wife, Sherry, and I conducted a spiritual journey to the Big Island of Hawaii. To begin the journey we conducted a spiritual/religious ceremony called a "burning" or "feeding the spirits of the ancestors." In other words, a *blót*. The ceremony was performed the day before my vision at dusk. In the predawn hours, less than twelve hours later, I experienced the divine call both as something heard and something seen—in the form of a vision and a voice. "This star is you; you are this star; the purification is of the people; all are one."

The next morning at the Big Island's White Sand Beach, my native Hawaiian healer friend gave me a message from one of his ancestors who came to him during the burning. "My ancestor brought me a message, but it's for you. My ancestor said that you are a kahuna *po'o* (high priest). You are a prophet bringing back first knowledge—the lost knowledge and sacred teachings that have been misunderstood, forgotten, and corrupted. You have a message, path, and way to share with this world, but do not identify it as being from these islands or other lands. This only separates people and does not unite them. Name it whatever you like. Don't get discouraged with the resistance you will face; it's your destiny."

The name I chose was Divine Humanity. All things are divine with the spark—the starlight of God, the Great Mystery, the All—within them. In other words, the divine is within all things (seen and unseen), and all things are within the divine. In Norse terms, Allfather is the same as *divine*. This is radical nonduality or oneness where spirit and matter, the absolute and relative, interpenetrate. And there is no original sin, only original divinity.

The oneness of interpenetrative radical nonduality sees a reality where there is no separation between mind and body, dark and light, or spirit and matter. The most profound and essential nature of things is not distinct from the things recognizable by our senses. In other words, our sacred self and our profane self are nondual and interpenetrate; likewise, all other sentient beings' (and things') sacred identity and profane identity are nondual and interpenetrate. This is true oneness.

Divine Humanity believes that each and every person has an immortal spark within them—an indestructible seed of divine light, the divine immanence. This indestructible seed of divine light may be likened to a mustard seed within our hearts or may be called Óðinn's seed.

⚜

Please use common sense. There are eight billion plus galaxies. Within each, there are an unknown number, probably billions, of stars. This is known creation. The earth sits in the corner of one of these galaxies—the Milky Way. It is the height of folly and arrogance that any human being or religious institution would have intimate knowledge and be able to identify and label the Creator of our known universe within their concrete of dogma and doctrine.

In fact, the dogmatic and doctrinal issue of "my god versus your god" has caused an unknown amount of suffering and bloodshed over the millennia.

I acknowledge that the Creator, the Unknown, the Uncreated, cannot be identified or imagined in human terms, just in absolute terms, as it is the greatest mystery of all mysteries. I use the term God when referring to the Absolute, the All.

However, I am not referring to the concept of the Christian God—the Father, Son, and the Holy Ghost—but to the Creator, the greatest Mystery of Mysteries, the Divine, the All, the Absolute, the Concealed and the Revealed, which is both immanent and transcendent and beyond human comprehension.

Thus, the one and oneness of all, which is within us and that is outside of us, transcends our abilities even as divine human beings to comprehend the essence of what is the greatest mystery of all. God surpasses our dualistic view of reality and is neither male nor female but is the mystery of all that there is. God is love not fear, both immanent and transcendent.

2. http://www.primordialtraditions.net/.

3. G. Philippe Menos and Karen A. Jones Menos, *Revelation and Inspiration: Paranormal Phenomena in Light of the Kundalini Paradigm*, May 21–23, 1989, 3.

4. Ralph Metzner, *The Well of Remembrance*, 218.

5. "The anatomy of individual brains varies in ways neuroscientists are only beginning to understand. Genes, environmental exposures, experience, and disease help wire our neurons differently." (Melissa Healy**,** *The Seattle Times*, Sunday, June 23, 2013, A7).

6. Neil McMahon, "Ásatrú: The old Norse religion practised by Iceland´s early Viking settlers," January 26 2015, http://icelandmag.com/article/asatru-old-norse-religion-practised-icelands-early-viking-settlers

7. Stefan Lovgren, *National Geographic News*, May 7, 2004 (http://news.nationalgeographic.com/news/2004/05/0507_040507_icelandsagas.html)

8. Jón Hnefill Aðalsteinsson, *A Piece of Horse Liver*, 17.

9. Rocco J. Gennaro, "Consciousness," *Internet Encyclopedia of Philosophy*, http://www.iep.utm.edu/consciou/.

10. Fundamental awakening is "a way of collapsing the distance between mind and enlightened mind, and thus, abolishing the dualism that is itself the stuff of delusion." (Bernard Faure, *Visions of Power*, 16.)

11. Charles D. Laughlin, http://www.scientificexploration.org/journal/jse_10_3_laughlin.pdf, p. 381

12. Even though Óðinn as Allfather may be a Christian addition, I feel it was based on older knowledge, primordial knowledge that fit the Christian image of one God.

13. The myths associated with Glastonbury Tor are extraordinary. It has been called a magic mountain, a faeries' glass hill, a spiral castle, a Grail castle, the Land of the Dead, Hades, a Druid initiation center, an Arthurian hill fort, a magnetic power point, a crossroads of leys, a place of goddess fertility rituals and celebrations, and a converging point for UFOs. (Frances Howard-Gordon, http://www.gothicimage.co.uk/books/makerofmyths1.html)

14. This poem is dedicated to the wounded raven that hobbled by my window one wintry afternoon.

15. Since the nineteenth century, "Important concepts of life were brought to the field of physiology such as homeostasis by Walter Cannon...Dr. Canon realized the importance of balance between acid and alkaline in the body fluids, especially in the blood...An acidic condition inhibits nerve action and an alkaline condition stimulates nerve action. One who has an alkaline blood condition can think and act (decide) well. On the other hand, one who has an acidic blood condition cannot think well or act quickly, clearly, or decisively...For a long time, I searched for a quick way to change an acidic to an alkaline condition. Finally, I found one through religious rituals. Japanese Shinto religion strongly recommends performing the misogi ritual, in which one takes a cold water bath or shower in a river, waterfall, or the ocean." (Herman Aihara, *Acid and Alkaline*, 1, 109).

16. Vince Stogan, modern-day John the Baptist, and his wife, Mom Stogan, were teachers to us and the primary elders of the First People of British Columbia. They were instrumental in bringing back their people's spirit dancing in the smokehouses. If you needed heavy-duty healing, it was Mom and Vince who you sought out. They were true shamans through and through; however, Vince didn't like to use that term and when pushed for a label, he would just say, "Call me an Indian doctor." Both he and Mom were the spiritual and religious leaders of their people. In fact,

Vince would probably object to my use of the term "religious leader," as organized religion was not his thing. Neither of these two of our beloved teachers still walk this earth.

17. Carole Cusack, "Pagan Saxon Resistance to Charlemagne's Mission: 'Indigenous' Religion and 'World' Religion in the Early Middle Ages, 9. (https://www.academia.edu/738533/Pagan_Saxon_Resistance_to_Charlemagne_s_Mission_Indigenous_Religion_and_World_Religion_in_the_Early_Middle_Ages)

18. Bil Linzie, *Investigating the Afterlife Concepts of the Norse Heathen: A Reconstructionist's Approach*, 21 (http://odroerirjournal.com/download/after_life_bil_linzie.pdf)

19. Vilhelm Grönbech, *The Culture of the Teutons*, 374.

20. Nancy B. Detweiler, *History of Astrology in Judaism & Christianity*, http://jhaines6.wordpress.com/2012/04/20/history-of-astrology-in-judaism-christianity-a-fantastic-article-that-helps-to-correct-some-of-our-false-history-j/.

21. Hilda Roderick Ellis, *The Road to Hel*, 139.

22. E. O. G. Turville-Petre, *Myth and Religion of the North*, 273.

23. Hilda Roderick Ellis, *The Road to Hel*, 149.

24. Ibid., 87.

25. Ibid., 199.

26. Vilhelm Grönbech, *The Culture of the Teutons*, 153.

27. K. R. Moore (2009) "Was Pythagoras Ever Really in Sparta?" Rosetta 6:1–25. Footnote 38, 10 http://www.rosetta.bham.ac.uk/issue6/pythagoras-sparta.pdf.

28. Paul Broadhurst, *Tintagel and the Arthurian Myths*, 99–100.

29. Malcolm Godwin, *Angels An Endangered Species*, 237.

30. Elisabeth Haich, *Wisdom of the Tarot*, 88.

31. Ibid., 89.

32. The symbol of the Sefirot is the defining notion of Kabbalistic theosophy. The Sefirot (singular Sefirah) which are almost always conceived to be ten in number, are the building blocks of creation, the archetypes of existence, the traits of God, and the primary values of the world. (http://www.newkabbalah.com/sefirot.html)

33. The tenth Sefirot means kingdom or Shekhina (Feminine divine presence).

34. Elisabeth Haich, *Wisdom of the Tarot*, 89.

35. The complete story of the Visitation is recorded in *Do You Like Jesus—Not the Church?*.

36. Sallie Nichols, *Angels and Mortals*, 190.

37. Beatrix Murrell, http://www.bizcharts.com/stoa_del_sol/plenum/plenum_3.html.

38. Ibid.

39. Ibid.

40. Bohm's theory of the implicate order stresses that the cosmos is in a state of process. Bohm's cosmos is a "feedback" universe that continuously recycles forward into a greater mode of being and consciousness. Ibid.

41. One of our apprentices took a picture of me during the day while we finished building the stone death spiral. No one saw what the camera picked

up. The picture is not of columns of light. It is an intense and immense light off to my left in the woods with two globes of light suspended above. The light has a shape almost like a sword in its center, with golden rays coming off it. It's been verified that it is not a reflection of the lens of the instant camera that took the picture.

42. Julius Evola, *The Mystery of the Grail*, p. xii

43. Joseph Campbell, *The Power of Myth*, 23.

44. Ibid., 55.

45. Douglas Forell Hulmes, *Sacred Trees of Norway and Swede: A Friluftsliv Quest*, 4.

46. Elsa-Britta Titchenell, *The Masks of Odin*, 3.

47. Jason Jeffrey, http://www.amerika.org/texts/hyperborea-and-the-quest-for-mystical-enlightenment-jason-jeffrey.

48. Usually, "as below, so above" means the heavens above are a reflection of us and "as above, so below" means that we are a reflection of the heavens imprinted at birth by our soul. As used by the author of this quote, "as below, as above" refers to our reflection of the underworld aspects of our darkness within which may take the form of growth and creativity or destructive patterns from our dysfunctional darkness—this is the realm of the beast, which I discuss later on in this book.

49. John Opsopaus, *Guide to the Pythagorean Tarot*, 192.

50. Fred Hageneder, *The Meaning of Trees*, 203.

51. http://www.greatdreams.com/three/three.htm.

52. Rudolf Simek, *Dictionary of Northern Mythology*, 40.

53. Ibid., 250.

54. Ibid., 40.

55. Ibid., 231.

56. Ibid., 231.

57. This knowledge demonstrates the importance of our feet, the need to spend time barefoot on the earth, less time in shoes, and the validity of reflexology.

58. To the majority of Christians, the Bible is not mythic but literal truth— the Word of God.

59. Maria Kvilhaug, http://freya.theladyofthelabyrinth.com/?page_id=76.

60. Elsa-Britta Titchenell, *The Masks of Odin*, 46.

61. Divine Humanity acknowledges that the Creator cannot be identified or imagined by the human mind and cannot be put into human terms, just in absolute terms, as it is the greatest Mystery of all Mysteries. The Absolute—the All, which Divine Humanity refers to as God, is beyond form and conception—the un-manifest. It is outside of time and space; in a sense it is timelessness.

    For reasons beyond what any human mind may comprehend, the Absolute reflected itself—the Reflective Absolute. From the Absolute and its Reflection, Reflective Absolute, was "birthed the duality that was nondual"—a void that was not void. Divine Humanity refers to the Absolute and the Reflective Absolute as the **Great Silence** (the sound of the Hebrew letter Aleph is silence) and the duality that was nondual as the **Dark Ocean**—containing the Eternal Male and Eternal Female.

    The reflective absolute (divine mind/consciousness) now interpenetrates this voidless void (Dark Ocean) and creation occurs. The Great Silence (divine mind/consciousness) has interpenetrated the Dark Ocean and the divine is now in triple aspect (divine mind/consciousness, divine spark in the "dark," divine spark in the "light"). From this the reflective absolute in triple aspect and the Dark Ocean birthed the Great Sea—the relative universe (seen and unseen). The Great Sea has wave action or vibration. With this the absolute is nondual to the relative, spirit is nondual to matter, divine is nondual to humanity (all things, seen and unseen of creation—Mother Nature). The divine is in all things and all things are in the divine. In other words, spirit is within matter, and matter is within spirit, all mutually penetrate. Thus, reality is interpenetrating radical nonduality—oneness. There is no separation between the absolute and the relative, between dark and light, spirit and matter, or between mind and body. Consciousness permeates and interpenetrates all reality. God is both immanent and transcendent. This may be likened to the realization through religious intuition of the essential oneness of the macrocosm and microcosm. Furthermore, the macrocosm, the universe/ Mother Nature, and oneself are essentially one.

62. Elsa-Britta Titchenell, *The Masks of Odin*, 46.

63. E. O. G. Turville-Petre, *Myth and Religion of the North*, 1.

64. Ralph Metzner, *The Well of Remembrance*, 200.

65. Ralph Metzner, *The Well of Remembrance*, 200.

66. "According to Nordic cosmology, Utgardr is the area outside the part of the world inhabited by gods and men (Asgard and Midgard respectively)." Rudolf Simek, *Dictionary of Northern Mythology*, 343.

67. Rudolf Simek, *Dictionary of Northern Mythology*, 20.

68. http://forums.philosophyforums.com/threads/knowledge-intuitive-andor-discursive-9297.html.

69. http://www.germanicmythology.com/original/cosmology2.html.

70. Rudolf Simek, *Dictionary of Northern Mythology*, 90.

71. Maria Kvilhaug, *The Seed of Yggdrasill*, 435.

72. Ibid., 368.

73. Ibid., 362.

74. Passions are anything that disturbs the tranquility of our mind.

75. Jürg Glauser and Susanne Kramarz-Bein (Hrsg.), Strengleikar in Iceland. 2014. Rittersagas: Übersetzung, Überlieferung, Transmission, 119–131, 127 (https://www.academia.edu/10666162/Strengleikar_in_Iceland._2014._Rittersagas_%C3%9Cbersetzung_%C3%9Cberlieferung_Transmission_pp._119_131).

76. See chapter 7 - Óðinn.

77. Stephan Grundy, *The Cult of Óðinn: God of Death*, 179.

78. Ibid., 178–179.

79. A great visual example of this is depicted in the movie *Emerald Forest*.

80. The following is an account of an exorcism of a spirit in the form of a serpent I performed on one of our apprentices in 1997 after the visitation—in her own words:

"From the start it was a strange injury. I do several sports; karate, where I was a purple belt, and tennis, which I play competitively at the club level. And so I always have plenty of opportunities to get injured. But I didn't get injured playing sports. I didn't even get injured within several days of doing one of my sports. I just woke up one morning and my heel hurt. Within two days my leg started to hurt, and within hours of the second day I couldn't put any weight onto my leg at all. I had ruptured my calf muscle. Recovery involved about six weeks in an air cast and physical therapy that included everything from swimming to special stretches.

"After about three months, I began returning slowly to my sports. After about nine months, I was back fully to my sports. There was, however, a nagging tightness and sometimes aching in my leg that never seemed to fully leave me. After a strenuous workout, it would even develop spasms, and at times I had full range of motion and didn't seem to be hindered sports-wise other than the discomfort, so I knew that something else was going on. I spoke to J. C. and asked if he would do a healing on my leg.

"Early one August morning, after a very powerful baptism ceremony, J. C. performed the healing. I don't know what energy he was tapping into; I did feel tingling up and down my spine. It was excruciatingly painful when he put his hands on my leg and pulled off whatever it was he was pulling off. That night when everyone had gone to bed at my house, I went into my meditation room to do some chanting and ceremony. My chanting kept getting interrupted because I felt like snakes were crawling over my body. I knew from the rational world that there were no snakes in my room in my house. But they felt so real that I couldn't concentrate. Finally, after several fruitless attempts, I decided to call it a night. As I was closing up my altar, I suddenly heard a very distinctive hissing sound coming from the corner of the room. I couldn't see anything, but the noise had a distinctly otherworldly feel to it. It made the hair on the back of my neck stand on end, and my blood instantly ran cold. It was paralyzing. I ran out of the room, closed the door, and called J. C. even though it was near midnight. Normally J. C. and his wife have an answering machine on so they do not have to answer the phone at night. But on this night J. C. had fallen asleep downstairs by the phone and had gotten up and was standing by the phone when it rang at midnight. I remember sobbing to him that something was hissing at me and I was terrified. J. C. said that he had taken a serpent off of my leg that morning and had cast it away, but sometimes this serpent energy will follow the person and 'stalk' him or her. He taught me a secret mudra (a hand position), a mantra (a vocalization or prayer), and a movement to chase it away.

"When I touched the doorknob of the room, I immediately felt the same cold horror. My hair stood up, and my blood felt chilled again. I walked carefully into the room with my arms crossed in front of me and my hands tightly holding onto the mudra. In the corner where the energy was most intense, I performed the combined movement and mantra twice.

"Immediately, my blood warmed up and the fear dissipated. Since this time, my leg has been wonderful. Other than occasional bouts of stiffness, I am able to move much more energetically, and I can feel the energy flow has returned to its normal levels. I am very grateful."

81.   Mircea Eliade, The Forge and the Crucible, 106.

82.   Anders Andrén, Kristina Jennbert, Catharina Raudvere (EDS), *Old Norse religion in long-term perspectives – Origins, Changes, and Interactions*: Henning Kure, *Hanging on the world tree*, 69.

83.   The Jellingestenene runic stones are located on the South side of the Jelling Church in the town of Jelling in Eastern Jutland. The runic stones, the two mounds and the first church were all raised and built in the 10 th century AD. Jelling and the historical monuments have been symbols of the founding of Denmark and the Danish monarchy.

The large Jellingesten, known as King Harald's Stone, is King Harald Bluetooth's statement to the World that he united Denmark and Norway into a single kingdom, and he claims to have converted the Danes to Christianity, which may to some degree have been a declaration of commitment rather than a statement of fact.

The depiction of Christ on King Harald's Stone is the oldest such picture found in Denmark. This is not a suffering Jesus Christ, but a triumphant Christ entwined in the branches of the Tree Of Life. (http://www.viking-denmark.com/jellingestenene-jelling-jylland-denmark.html)

84. Anders Andrén, Kristina Jennbert, Catharina Raudvere (EDS), *Old Norse religion in long-term perspectives – Origins, Changes, and Interactions*: Henning Kure, *Hanging on the world tree*, 71.

85. As in Shintoism: special ropes (*shimenawa*) and strips of white paper (*gohei*).

86. Sebastian L. Klein, *The Christianization of the Norse c.900-c.1100*, 2011, 49-50. (https://www.academia.edu/1154617/Christianizing_the_Norse_c.900-c.1100_A_Premeditated_Strategy_of_Life_and_Death_PDF_version_)

87. Acharya S/D. M. Murdock, http://www.freethoughtnation.com/contributing-writers/63-acharya-s/666-ancient-unparalleled-pre-christian-temple-discovered-in-norway.html.

88. Hanne Christiansen, *Inside Iceland's pagan revival*, March, 2015, (http://www.dazeddigital.com/artsandculture/article/24321/1/inside-icelands-pagan-revival?utm_source=Link&utm_medium=Link&utm_campaign=RSSFeed&utm_term=inside-icelands-pagan-reviva)

89. Neil McMahon, *Iceland's Asatru pagans reach new height with first temple*, 14 February 2015, (http://www.bbc.com/news/world-europe-31437973)

90. Dawn M. Shiley, http://www.catscenterstage.com/breeds/norwegian-forest-cat2.shtml.

91. Elsa-Brita Titchenell, *The Masks of Odin*, p. 27

92. Ibid., excerpted 27–28.

93. Eric Wódening, *We Are Our Deeds*, 67–68.

94. Ibid., 69–70.

95. This concept of the Kingdom of Óðinn (Allfather) is identical to the concept of the Kingdom of God with God not being the Christian God but the absolute principle within all things.

96. Joseph Campbell, *The Power of Myth*, 31.

97. Ibid., 22.

98. http://en.wikipedia.org/wiki/Frigg.

99. Rudolf Simek, *Dictionary of Northern Mythology*, 250.

100. William P. Reaves, *The Cult of Freyr and Freyja*, 3.

101. Vilhelm Grönbech, *The Culture of the Teutons*, 124.

102. Ibid., 141.

103. Ibid., 162.

104. Ibid., 372.

105. Ibid., 150.

106. Ibid., 150.

107. Ibid., 35.

108. Ibid., 75.

109. Ibid., 75.

110. Ibid., 129.

111. Shelley M. White, "Heart Based Consciousness: Using The Heart As An Organ Of Perception," April 10, 2015 (http://www.collective-evolution.com/

2015/04/10/heart-based-consciousness-using-the-heart-as-an-organ-of-perception/)

112. More recently, it was discovered that the heart also secretes oxytocin, commonly referred to as the 'love' or bonding hormone. (http://www.healthwithconfidence.com/heart-hormones.html)

113. Edred Thorsson, *Runelore*, 43.

114. Hilda Roderick Ellis, *The Road to Hel*, 117.

115. Rudolf Simek, *Dictionary of Northern Mythology*, 186.

116. Andreas Kornevall, "The Norse Legend of the World Tree—Yggdrasil," February 15, 2015, http://www.ancient-origins.net/myths-legends-europe/norse-legend-world-tree-yggdrasil-002680.

117. Amanda Froelich, "Science Proves Hugging Trees Is Good for Health," June 23, 2014, http://www.trueactivist.com/science-proves-hugging-trees-is-good-for-health/.

118. The number one symbolizes the Absolute, the One, the Divine, the Great Mystery, the Creator. The number ten symbolized the reflection of the Divine or the perfection of creation. "In the number 10 creation reaches perfection and fulfillment. The masculine-positive, creative principle of God has penetrated and fertilized space, the negative, maternal aspect, and has become one with it." (Elisabeth Haich, *Wisdom of the Tarot*, 88.)

119. Hilda Roderick Ellis, *The Road to Hel*, 127.

120. Ibid., 129.

121. Ibid., 131.

122. Vilhelm Grönbech, *The Culture of the Teutons*, 159.

123. Anna Morduch, *The Sovereign Adventure*, 185.

124. Since the nineteenth century, "important concepts of life were brought to the field of physiology such as homeostasis by Walter Cannon... Dr. Canon realized the importance of balance between acid and alkaline in the body fluids, especially in the blood...An acidic condition inhibits nerve action and an alkaline condition stimulates nerve action. One who has an alkaline blood condition can think and act (decide) well. On the other hand, one who has an acidic blood condition cannot think well or act quickly, clearly, or decisively...For a long time, I searched for a quick way to change an acidic to an alkaline condition. Finally, I found one through religious rituals. Japanese Shinto religion strongly recommends performing the misogi ritual, in which one takes a cold water bath or shower in a river, waterfall, or the ocean." Herman Aihara, *Acid and Alkaline*, 1, 109.

125. Hilda Roderick Ellis, *The Road to Hel*, 75.

126. Ibid., 75.

127. Anders Andrén, Kristina Jennbert, Catharina Raudvere (EDS), *Old Norse religion in long-term perspectives – Origins, Changes, and Interactions*: Andres Siegfried Dobat, *Bridging mythology and belief*, 186.

128. Ibid., 186.

129. Thomas A. DuBois, *Nordic Religions in the Viking Age*, 79.

130. Vilhelm Gronbech, *The Culture of the Teutons*, 378.

131. Elsa-Britta Titchenell, *The Masks of Odin*, 39.

132. Vilhelm Gronbech, *The Culture of the Teutons*, 148.

133. Ibid., 150.

134. Douglas Lockhart, *Jesus the Heretic*, 339.

135. Rudolf Simek, *Dictionary of Northern Mythology*, 107.

136. Jón Hnefill Aðalsteinsson, *A Piece of Horse Liver*, 24.

137. Rudolf Simek, *Dictionary of Northern Mythology*, 107.

138. Light-emitting diodes are unique in producing white light. This is due to the fact that the electric current (negative and positive) itself is the light, unlike incandescent bulbs, which use electricity to produce a glowing filament that emits light, or fluorescent lights, which use a glowing gas to produce light.

    The birth of light-emitting diodes only came after the creation of blue diodes. Up until that time, the only diodes available were red and green, and without a blue diode, white light cannot be created. When red, green, and blue diodes are combined and "an electric field is applied, negative and positive charges meet in the middle layer and combine to produce photons of light." In other words, with the blending or interpenetration of negative and positive or, if you will, symbolic spirit and matter, light is produced. The magic of LEDs reflects the magic of radical nonduality. When we awaken to a consciousness of radical nonduality, we awaken our dormant sparks; our divine light awakens and begins the process of evolving into a body of light. (Rev. Dr. JC Husfelt, *Do You Like Jesus—Not the Church*, 215 - 216)

139. http://starryskies.com/The_sky/events/meteors/thunderstones-shootingstars.html.

140. Jonathan Z. Smith, *The HarperCollins Dictionary of Religion*, 392.

141. Vilhelm Grönbech, *The Culture of the Teutons*, 90.

142. Ibid., 89.

143. Ibid., 90.

144. Ibid., 94.

145. Ibid., 161.

146. Ibid., 153.

147. http://www.umich.edu/~umfandsf/symbolismproject/symbolism.html/F/fire.html.

148. Ibid.

149. Anders Andrén, Kristina Jennbert, Catharina Raudvere (EDS), *Old Norse religion in long-term perspectives – Origins, Changes, and Interactions*: Randi Barndon, *Myth and metallurgy*, 99.

150. Wyrd Designs, "Loki: At the Hearth Fire," http://www.patheos.com/blogs/pantheon/2010/06/wyrd-designs-loki-at-the-hearth-fire/.

151. Ibid.

152. Tony van Renterghem, *When Santa Was a Shaman*, 4.

153. Ibid., 4.

154. Elsa-Brita Titchenell, *The Masks of Odin*, 126.

155. Ibid., 36.

156. Ibid., 37.

157. http://en.wikipedia.org/wiki/Bl%C3%B3t.

158. Vilhelm Grönbech, *The Culture of the Teutons*, 346.

159. Ibid., 351.

160. Ritual consists of one or two individuals; ceremony consists of three or more people.

161. Vilhelm Grönbech, *The Culture of the Teutons*, 331–332.

162. Daniel Bray, *Sacrifice and Sacrificial Ideology in Old Norse Religion*, 127–128.

163. Vilhelm Grönbech, *The Culture of the Teutons*, 374.

164. Ibid., 373.

165. Rudolf Simek, *Dictionary of Northern Mythology*, 322.

166. Diana L. Paxson, *Taking Up The Runes*, 185–186.

167. There are many was of telling this fine tale. One of them has found its way to my hall and step. When I heard it, it was from an old woman, a Helja Runar (another name for Erulian) who told me many stories of the old ways. And though this may not be the exact retelling of more famous poets, each story is told in its own way, each story possessing truths of its own. So I warn you thus, if this story is not like the one you have heard, do not dispute a dead woman's words, but take it as a simple story of old from a different point of view.—Spaerunn Helgardar (http://dessyvamp.deviantart.com/journal/A-Tale-Of-Fenrir-273484156)

168. http://thenorsegods.com/.

169. The original word was lion, I changed to wolf, which has the same meaning as: "Jesus said: Blessed is the lion which the man eats and the lion will become man; and cursed is the man whom the lion eats and the lion will become man." (Rev. Dr. JC Husfelt, *Do You Like Jesus – Not the Church?*, 96)

170. "Jung appeared to be undecided in his own mind about the question of the ontological status of the archetypes (see e.g., 1968d [1936], 58; see also Dourley, 1993); and this state of affairs has led to considerable controversy. But I believe that the ambiguity was necessitated by Jung's inability to scientifically reconcile his conviction that the archetypes are at once embodied structures and bear the imprint of the divine; that is, the archetypes are both structures within the human body, and represent the domain of spirit. Jung's intention was clearly a unitary one, and yet his ontology seemed often to be dualistic, as well as persistently ambiguous, and was necessarily, so because the science of his day could not envision a nondualistic conception of spirit and matter.

"Jung's dualism is apparent in his distinction between the archetypes and the instincts which required for him a polarization of the psyche into those products derived from matter and those derived from spirit. He imagined the psyche as the intersection at the apex of two cones, one of spirit and the other of matter (1969a [1946], 215)."

Charles D. Laughlin, http://www.scientificexploration.org/journal/jse_10_3_laughlin.pdf.

171. Diana L. Paxson, *Taking Up the Runes*, 185.

172. This is connected to the concept that our conscious minds consistently seek power. The definition of power is individualistic. In our society, most people equate power with external, materialistic things, such as status, position, title, money, possessions, and even physical attractiveness; consider the amount of cosmetic surgery and the money spent on cosmetics.

173. *Seattle Times*, November 21, 2010, A19.

174. Vilhelm Grönbech, *The Culture of the Teutons*, 139.

175. If we were to ask the average New Age practitioner the meaning of *chakra*, the response would probably be "energy vortexes" or "energy wheels." That would be correct if we are talking about the exoteric meaning. But

what many do not know is the original esoteric meaning. The original name meant "discus," as in the lethal throwing weapon, with the meaning of destroying the passions that hinder a person's journey toward enlightenment. *Passions* means anything that disrupts the tranquility of the mind.

The common number of chakras is seven. However, some systems of thought may have five or eight. It is believed that chakras are depositories of memory. Our emotional woundings and the past issues connected with those woundings may be locked away within the various chakras. These blockages will definitely affect and inhibit the energy flow throughout our body. Over time, this disharmony will affect the body's various health systems, such as the organs and glands and will ultimately result in a state of unhappiness and disease.

The first chakra is the root chakra. It is located at the base of the spine and deals with issues of security, basic needs, basic human survival, profane sex, inappropriate sexual activity (unawakened beast), and one's sense of roots and family and connection to the earth (an unawakened first chakra views earth/nature as hostile). This is the chakra of dualism, the endocrine system, the reproductive glands, and the adrenals. The color is red.

176. http://www.viking-glima.com/berserkers.html.

177. Anatoly Liberman, *In Prayer and Laughter Essays on Medieval Scandinavian and Germanic Mythology, Literature, and Culture*, 109.

178. Ibid., 110.

179. Ibid., 108.

180. http://grapevine.is/news/2015/03/20/celebrating-the-solar-eclipse-at-the-viking-temple/.

181. Elsa-Brita Titchenell, *The Masks of Odin*, 74–77.

182. E. O. G. Turville-Petre, *Myth and Religion of the North*, 58.

183. Ibid., 60.

184. Timothy Bourns, "The Language of Birds in Old Norse Tradition," 30, http://skemman.is/stream/get/1946/12869/31219/1/The_Language_of_Birds_in_Old_Norse_Tradition.pdf.

185. Ibid., 31–32.

186. E. O. G. Turville-Petre, *Myth and Religion of the North*, 49.

187. It seems that the timing is perfect to educate people on seiðr, as the seventh episode of Star Wars is titled *The Force Awakens*.

188. Counterclockwise.

189. Terry Gunnell, "'Magical Mooning' and the 'Goatskin Twirl': 'Other' Kinds of Female Magical Practices in Early Iceland," 137 (https://www.academia.edu/10458309/_Magical_Mooning_and_the_Goatskin_Twirl_Magical_Practices).

190. Mindy MacLeod and Bernard Mees, *Runic Amulets and Magic Objects*, 15.

191. Incantation also refers to chanting. Mantras are Buddhism's chants. One of the best known is Mahāyāna Buddhism Heart Sutra. A lesser-known chant is the lesser spell of the Shingon Esoteric Buddhist deity Fudō-myōō. These chants have a singing quality to them and provide insight into galdr.

192. http://en.wikipedia.org/wiki/Galdr.

193. Andy Orchard, *The Elder Edda: A Book of Viking Lore*, 37.

194. Ibid., 39.

195. Elsa-Brita Titchenell, *The Masks of Odin*, 126.

196. Mindy MacLeod and Bernard Mees, *Runic Amulets and Magic Objects*, 5.

197. Ibid., 4.

198. Ibid., 79–80.

199. Ibid., 8.

200. Edred Thorsson, *Alu*, 9.

201. Mindy MacLeod and Bernard Mees, *Runic Amulets and Magic Objects*, 89.

202. Ibid., 137.

203. Neil McMahon, "Ásatrú: The old Norse religion practised by Iceland´s early Viking settlers," Jan 26 2015, http://icelandmag.com/article/asatru-old-norse-religion-practised-icelands-early-viking-settlers.

204. The Dark Mountain Project is a network of writers, artists and thinkers who have stopped believing the stories our civilisation tells itself. We see that the world is entering an age of ecological collapse, material contraction and social and political unravelling, and we want our cultural responses to reflect this reality rather than denying it.

 The Project grew out of a feeling that contemporary literature and art were failing to respond honestly or adequately to the scale of our entwined ecological, economic and social crises. We believe that writing and art have a crucial role to play in coming to terms with this reality, and in questioning the foundations of the world in which we find ourselves. (http://dark-mountain.net/about/the-dark-mountain-project/)

205. Ibid.

www.ingramcontent.com/pod-product-compliance
Lightning Source LLC
LaVergne TN
LVHW020055090426
835513LV00029B/1524